WOMEN ARTISTS
IN HISTORY
FROM ANTIQUITY
TO THE 20TH CENTURY

Wendy Slatkin

*University of California,
Riverside*

WOMEN ARTISTS IN HISTORY

FROM ANTIQUITY TO THE 20TH CENTURY

Prentice-Hall, Inc., Englewood Cliffs, New Jersey 07632

Library of Congress Cataloging in Publication Data

SLATKIN. WENDY.
    Women artists in history.

    Bibliography: p.
    Includes index.
    1. Women artists—Biography. 1. Title.
N43.S57 1985   709'.2'2 [B]   84-11481
ISBN   0-13-961821-X

Editorial/production supervision and
    interior design: Chrystena Chrzanowski
Cover design: Diane Saxe
Manufacturing buyer: Harry P. Baisley

Printed in the United States of America

10   9   8   7   6   5   4   3   2   1

ISBN   0-13-961821- X   01

PRENTICE-HALL INTERNATIONAL, INC., *London*
PRENTICE-HALL OF AUSTRALIA PTY. LIMITED, *Sydney*
EDITORA PRENTICE-HALL DO BRASIL, LTDA., *Rio de Janeiro*
PRENTICE-HALL CANADA INC., *Toronto*
PRENTICE-HALL OF INDIA PRIVATE LIMITED, *New Delhi*
PRENTICE-HALL OF JAPAN, INC., *Tokyo*
PRENTICE-HALL OF SOUTHEAST ASIA PTE. LTD., *Singapore*
WHITEHALL BOOKS LIMITED, *Wellington, New Zealand*

In memory of my sister
GAIL SLATKIN ORNSTEIN
(1944–1982)

Contents

6

Eighteenth-Century Italian and French Painters   *67*

7

Neoclassical Painters and Sculptors   *81*

8

Introduction to the Modern Era   *92*

9

Painters in France: 1850–1900   *97*

10

Early Twentieth-Century Artists *114*

11

Artists of the Post-World War II Era *142*

Preface

Women Artists in History: From Antiquity to the 20th Century provides an overview of the accomplishments of women artists throughout recorded history. The careers of approximately forty creators, mostly painters and sculptors, are discussed and illustrated. However, photography is widely accepted in both academic circles and the culture at large as art, begging for the necessary inclusion of a group of women vitally important to the history of photography. Finally, the undeniably sophisticated formal and technical products of the medieval embroiderers of *opus anglicanum* and American quiltmakers argued for discussion of their artistic importance.

An understanding of the achievements of these artists is impossible without some information about the cultural milieu in which they lived and worked. Therefore, *Women Artists in History* also includes introductory material for each successive historical epoch, focusing on the social, economic, and demographic factors that have direct bearing on women's potential to become professional artists.

We know that women have been making art since earliest recorded history, and the number of practicing professional women artists has increased steadily since the Renaissance. This growing body of professionals is reflected in the larger number of artists included in this text who lived in the nineteenth and twentieth centuries. This may be explained by concomitant improvements in access to education and more egalitarian legal and economic rights for women. Quite simply, as western civilization lifted restrictions placed on women, more of them became viable artists.

Most important, each artist's contribution to and position in the history of art is defined. Unlike most published treatments of this topic, I have resisted the temptation to record women artists of mere competence. The artists selected for discussion in this text have each made a unique, significant contribution to the history of art and have survived a rigorous selection process, comparable to the criteria applied to male artists for inclusion in survey texts. These criteria, discussed in the introduction, include technical or formal innovations, iconographic originality, artistic influence, and status in the contemporary culture. The responsibility for these selections is wholly mine.

In the interest of comprehensibility, I have tried to organize discussions of each artist around the works illustrated in the text. When appropriate, I draw comparisons with the works of a male colleague whose art may not be reproduced. Wherever this occurs, the male artist's work is reproduced in any standard art history survey textbook.

The artists analyzed in *Women Artists in History* are not presented with the implication that they are the only women artists worthy of attention or wider recognition. Nor does this book ever make a case for a specifically "feminine" style in art. It is sincerely hoped that readers will be stimulated to explore the subject in greater depth. Therefore, suggestions for further reading are provided in the annotated bibliography that appears at the end of the text. Instructors may also find these suggestions helpful, for users of this text will invariably need to modify and expand its contents to fit their specific purposes.

Inspiration for this text originally came in the spring of 1980 when I was teaching both a standard art history survey course and a specialized course on women artists at Rutgers University in Camden, N.J. At that time, I became acutely aware that there was no extant textbook that bridged the artificial gender divisions between male and female artists in history; in fact, virtually no women artists were included in the most widely used survey textbooks. (Newer editions of such texts are rectifying these earlier omissions.) It therefore seemed very clear to me that a textbook correcting this imbalance and restoring the reputations of the most outstanding women artists was urgently needed. Fortunately, investigation into the careers of many women artists already had begun. This book rests on a body of scholarly research, led by the brilliant efforts of Ann Sutherland Harris and Linda Nochlin, authors of *Women Artists: 1550–1950*. Their volume was the catalogue for an exhibition that aroused great excitement as it toured the country in 1976.

Women Artists in History was designed to disseminate much of this existing scholarship and to educate a broader public to the existence of a group of outstanding women artists. Envisioned primarily as a supplemental textbook for college students in introductory art history courses, it should also prove useful to those enrolled in studio art, art appreciation, history of women artists, and other women's studies courses. Artists and other art professionals may utilize the text to expand their knowledge of the major issues concerning the historical position of women artists. Finally, interested general readers will find *Women Artists in History* accessible and informative.

Many people have contributed to the creation of this book. My students, responsive and enthusiastic, have always encouraged me to write for their needs. Diane Kirkpatrick carefully scrutinized the manuscript, and many of her suggestions have been incorporated into the text. Ruth Butler provided assistance in the final organization of the chapters. Estelle Fuchs contributed to the section on women in prehistory, and Janet Kaplan wrote the text on the Surrealists, improving my comments tremendously. Susan Weiss worked to obtain permissions needed for illustrations, and Pat-

Art and the Position of Women in Society

The history of women artists cannot consist simply in the biographical accounts of the achievements of a few exceptional women who changed the course of art history. It is difficult to appreciate the significance of these important individuals without a knowledge of the options available to them in any given historical epoch or culture. The fundamental roles, restrictions, or liberties permitted to women in their societies is essential information for an understanding of the ways in which women could participate in the making of art—or the ways in which they were excluded from such activities.

In every epoch, demographic factors directly affect women's ability to engage in productive or creative work. The most basic consideration, of course, is survival. In some cultures, such as ancient Greece where female infanticide was routinely practiced, fewer female babies were raised to maturity. Another factor is the age at which a woman is married and the proportion of women in the population who do marry. When women are married by age fifteen, they can scarcely have time to acquire any professional skills. The average number of children a woman bears, the size of her household, and the nature of her family responsibilities also directly affect the amount of time she can devote to creative work. A woman who has numerous pregnancies and is responsible for the care of a large family will certainly have difficulty finding time to practice a skilled activity like painting. Not surprisingly, the output of many women artists falls off after marriage. Such factors also affected the life expectancy of women in the past because women often died in childbirth. As late as the early 1900s, the painter Paula Modersohn-Becker died prematurely after the birth of a daughter. To maintain proper perspective, then, in this text each of the historical epochs is introduced with demographic information. It is not coincidental that the nineteenth century, which witnessed both a decline in the birth rate and an increased proportion of unmarried women, saw a dramatic rise in the number of women artists. As the absolute numbers of practicing women professionals increase, so do the numbers of outstanding women artists who profoundly influence, and at times even change, the course of art history. By the twentieth century, women artists are participating in all major avant-garde movements, not in isolation but in groups.

In addition to marital age, child-rearing activities, and mortality rates, any given society has a set of political, legal, and economic rights and restrictions that directly affect a woman's ability to become a professional artist. Artists are, after all, one category of worker, and professional artists operate to a certain extent like other business or professional persons. To understand the role of women in the arts, it is necessary to know what economic and legal rights women held in their day, for example, whether or not they were legally permitted to practice a trade, become a member of a guild, run a business, sign contracts, appear as a witness in court, etc. Clearly, when women are forbidden such activities, it is difficult for them to become professional artists.

Another economic consideration, the social class to which a woman belonged, directly affected her options. Very often, societies have different sets of expectations and permissible behavior norms for women of different classes. It is often impossible to generalize about the women in a given culture because the class into which a woman is born may be a more significant factor than her sex in determining the possibility for her to become a practicing artist. While painting and drawing have been considered proper accomplishments for women of the upper class since the Middle Ages, gentlewomen were not permitted to practice these arts as serious, professional activities until the twentieth century.

In many cultures throughout history, women of the upper classes were virtually confined to their homes. Only activities related to the needs of the household were considered appropriate. Traditionally, women have been associated with the making of containers, such as baskets and pottery, for household use. Women also have been primarily responsible for the manufacture of textiles for use as clothing and the decoration of these garments, often with embroidery. Domestic activities of this nature are outside the realm of the "fine arts," which are public and professional, and fall more within the category of the "crafts" or the "decorative" or "minor" arts. Art history has traditionally focused exclusively upon the fine arts, i.e., painting, sculpture, and architecture, and has ignored the many creative outlets through which women have expressed their visual sensibilities, such as quilt design, which requires no formal training. One of the concerns of the feminist art movement of the 1970s was the renewed appreciation of women's creativity in craft media, especially the tradition of needlework.

Psychological factors undoubtedly also play a determining role. Every society projects ideal models for behavior. The social conditioning of women often differs from that of men. Some cultures have demanded that women be demure, self-effacing, docile, and obedient. These behavioral qualities, combined with the socioeconomic restrictions noted earlier, are not likely to encourage the professional excellence and independence needed for a woman to become an outstanding artist.

Furthermore, regardless of whether a woman possesses such characteristics, the practice of the fine arts is dependent on a lengthy period of training to achieve professional competence. In order to understand the role of women artists in art history, it is important to consider the availability of artistic training for young women of talent. Prior to the twentieth century, even the most talented women were handicapped by the inequality of opportunities for professional education. During the late Middle Ages, artists learned their crafts as apprentices and journeymen. Women were not permitted to become apprentices and were thus denied access to training. When art academies took over the role of the education of artists in the seventeenth and eighteenth centuries, women were not allowed to become students at these schools. Not until the late nineteenth century were women permitted to receive comparable artistic training.

Given the problems they encountered in obtaining a complete, professional education, it is not surprising that most women artists before the twentieth century were daughters of artists. Being born into an artist's family gave these women access to training at an early age, an advantage denied to creative or talented women who did not have artists for fathers. However, being trained by one's father was also a handicap to an artist in terms of her ability to develop an original style. All too often, daughters were forced to copy their fathers' compositions, and they were relegated, like the female members of other artisans' households, to the most menial tasks of the studio.

During the Renaissance, when historical subjects became the vogue, a knowledge of human anatomy was essential for an artist who wished to paint large-scale, multifigured compositions. Since women were explicitly forbidden to study the male nude, they rarely received important commissions. Unable to acquire complete artistic training on a par with men, women artists often settled for mere competence. Insecure with their skills, they rarely felt confident enough to create an innovative style.

The situation of women artists before 1800 has been aptly summed up by Harris:

> By and large, women did not attempt to compete with men for the more prestigious public commissions . . . very few women in any European country attempted large-scale historical or religious compositions until the nineteenth century. Their limited training confined most women to the less valued specialties of portraiture and still life. With very few exceptions, women did not even try landscape painting until the nineteenth century. . . . Thus men not only controlled the most remunerative and most esteemed public commissions as well as landscape, one of the three popular genres, but also had an almost total monopoly over sculpture, architecture, and even printmaking before 1800.[1]

The crucial importance of access to education is underscored by the difference in women's contributions to the field of photography as compared with architecture. Prior to the late nineteenth century, architects were always male. While a few women have acquired the training necessary to become practicing architects in the last hundred years, their achievements are not sufficiently original to warrant detailed discussion in this text. On the other hand, no formal training was required to become a photographer. And, because photography was not originally an art form, its technology was equally available to men and women. In chapter ten, we will meet a group of women who are among the most innovative and important photographers since the invention of the medium in the nineteenth century.

The artists selected for detailed discussion in this text are all exceptional. Through a variety of circumstances, these women overcame the obstacles to training and the preconceptions of their cultures to create a body of works that deserve recognition. The women artists included in this text have all made significant contributions to the history of art when judged by the traditional standards used in selecting male artists for such inclusion.

It is important to remember, however, that the vast majority of women artists remain unnamed in this book. This parallels the situation for male artists. Prior to the Renaissance, most artists, male and female, were anonymous. Works were rarely signed and virtually no biographical information on their creators has survived. Beginning in the fifteenth century, the identities of individual artists are preserved, along with more documentation about their lives and careers. Those who are included in the mainstream of art history are the truly extraordinary, singled out for excellence from the majority of practicing artists. That there are fewer women who rank as outstanding reflects the smaller number of practicing female artists in any specific epoch rather than an innately inferior creative capacity in women. This reduced population of practicing women artists is the result, in turn, of those biological and cultural factors noted earlier that limited women's ability to become professional artists.

The achievements of most of the artists who are discussed in detail in this book were recognized by their contemporaries, and that recognition was preserved throughout the nineteenth century. However, when art history became codified as an academic discipline in the twentieth century, the reputation of these artists became obscured. The making of art, as taught in our universities until quite recently, was identified exclusively with the activities of male artists: ". . . modern art history produces a picture of the history of art from which women are not only absent, but identifies women artists as inevitably and naturally artists of lesser talent and no historical significance."[2]

The absence of women in most traditional accounts of the history of Western art has led to an underlying assumption that women are not capable of excellence in the fine arts simply because they are women. The artists discussed in this text disprove that assumption. They have been selected for detailed discussion because they have made significant contributions to the history of art according to the following criteria:

1. *Stylistic or technical innovation.* A number of artists have developed methods of painting and sculpture that are different from any previous style. These artists usually are members of an avant-garde group. This category applies most frequently for artists living in the late nineteenth and twentieth centuries, when stylistic innovation has been most valued. However, Rosalba Carriera, for example, was a technical innovator in the lower-status categories of miniature painting and pastel portraiture during the eighteenth century.

2. *Compositional or iconographic originality.* Some artists have been singled out because they invented a new format, compositional arrangement, or structure for painting or sculpture. For example, the originality of Clara Peeters lies more in her compositions and the selected viewpoint of her still lifes than in her method of paint application. A number of artists have invented new subjects, sometimes based specifically on their experiences as women. Other artists have developed new variations or layers of meaning

for subjects regularly depicted by their male colleagues. Judith Leyster, Harriet Hosmer, and Käthe Kollwitz are examples of artists who have created new iconographies based on their personal identities as women.

3. *Influence on other artists.* One standard regularly applied by art historians to evaluate the contribution of an artist to the history of art is the extent to which he or she influenced other artists. The works of certain artists, such as Angelica Kauffman and Artemisia Gentileschi, exerted a decisive and widespread influence on the art of their contemporaries.

4. *Recognition within the culture.* Many of the artists to be discussed were widely appreciated during their lifetimes. Each received official and critical recognition and occupied positions of prominence in her contemporary culture. Rachel Ruysch, Elisabeth Vigée-Lebrun, and Rosa Bonheur are examples of artists whose careers belong in this category.

These criteria are clearly not mutually exclusive, and some artists to be discussed are noteworthy for more than one of them.

Women artists, like men artists, create within a given national and period framework. Therefore, it is necessary to view the works in this book within their historical context in the mainstream of art history. Being a woman is merely one factor, among many, that determines what type of art a person will create. It is for this reason that the works of art illustrated in this text display a broad range of styles and subjects, as this is appropriate for works created in different countries and diverse historical epochs.

There seems to be no validity, then, to generalizations about a "feminine" style as opposed to a "masculine" one. In fact, labeling an artist's work "feminine" is often an indirect way of assigning a negative value judgment to that work. "Feminine" art is said to possess "grace" and "delicacy" at the expense of "power" and "strength." "Feminine" artists select intimate domestic subjects, while "masculine" artists depict the heroic actions and events in which men participate. "Feminine" artists work on a small scale, which automatically excludes their works from "significance" in art historical terms. The works of women artists are often considered inferior in quality if they possess the traits that may be characterized by the term "feminine."

This study is also limited to the contributions of women creators in Western civilization. The artistic activities of women in Oriental cultures or African civilizations, for example, fall outside the scope of this discussion. Any generalizations that are made concerning "women artists" must therefore be understood as implicitly confined in this way.

Let us turn, then, to a historical account of women artists in history, leaving behind, as much as possible, any preconceptions we may have about them.

chapter 1

From Prehistory to the Roman Empire

The beginnings of Western civilization do not coincide with the earliest artifacts, the first known works of art, or the survival of written records. The historical era upon which we formulate our understanding of the past is a relatively recent epoch in human history. Thousands of years of social organization preceded the appearance of the already highly evolved civilizations of Sumer and Egypt in the third millennium, B.C.

The oldest known works of sculpture are statuettes of obese standing women with enlarged breasts and bellies. The famous *Venus of Willendorf* (Figure 1) is one of many such statuettes that have been discovered across the Eurasian continent. Some of these figures date from the neolithic era (ca. 25,000–20,000 B.C.) while others are as "late" as 5.000 B.C. A few statuettes have been found *in situ*, in shrines, and can therefore be assumed to represent a divinity or a votive offering to that divinity. From the evidence of these figures, one may postulate the worship of a mother goddess to ensure fertility.

However, the existence of these objects does not necessarily tell us about the organization of society, the division of labor between the sexes, or the relative status of women and men in communities of the prehistoric past. Such issues are continuing sources of speculation and scholarly controversy. Nonetheless, from the incontrovertible evidence of these numerous fertility images, one may deduce that "the female body was experienced in its own character as a focus of divine force and a system of rites was dedicated to its mystery."[1]

The survival of these fertility statuettes, as well as mythological references to them, have elicited many speculations about the existence in prehistoric culture of societies organized as matriarchies. There is no consensus among scholars that this was the case. On the contrary, "motherhood has often placed abstract *woman* on a pedestal, but it has at the same time left concrete *women* in the home and powerless.

FIGURE 1. *"Venus" of Willendorf.* c. 30,000–25,000 B.C.
Limestone. H.: 4 3/8". Naturhistorisches Museum, Vienna.

Reverence . . . does not necessarily result from, or lead to, the high status or power of the revered object that is symbolically presented."[2]

While contemporary anthropologists generally discount any arguments for the widespread existence of matriarchies in prehistory, some tribes may have been organized on a matrilineal basis. In matrilineal societies, inheritance takes place through the mother's line and children take their mother's name. Other cultures may have been matrilocal, i.e., the husband lives with the wife's family. Both matrilineal and matrilocal customs confer on women a measure of status and power within their cultures because kinship networks, economic status, and social rank are based on the person's relationship to the mother rather than the father.

That there are biological differences between men and women is clear and undeniable. But biology alone does not determine the roles, activities, and status differences between men and women in any given culture. "The chief importance of biological sex in determining social roles is in providing a universal and obvious division around which other distinctions can be organized."[3] Although every society has some sort of division of tasks by sex, the assignment of any particular task to one sex or the other varies enormously from culture to culture.

In the absence of concrete evidence, it is very difficult to determine the extent of women's participation in craft activity. We simply do not know whether women were responsible for the creation of fertility figurines, the making of clothing, or the fashioning of clay pots or woven baskets. Evidence from the Anatolian settlement of Çatal Hüyük, dating back to the seventh millenium B.C., indicates that this community was "unmistakably matrilineal and matrilocal"[4] and that women participated in food cultivation as well as hunting and gathering. Women made pottery and textiles, operating the oldest known looms. Such evidence is consistent with the activities of women in more modern hunting and gathering cultures. But whether women performed these tasks in prehistory remains purely conjectural.

In recent years, many anthropologists have accepted the theory that a stage of comparatively egalitarian economic and social organization preceded the patriarchal stratification of classes and cultures of the historic eras.[5] It is believed that humanity originally lived in small bands or tribes organized by kinship relations, in which property was owned communally. Archeological evidence of the earliest societies in Europe and the Mediterranean basin supports the theory of egalitarian communism in prehistoric cultures. Danubian I peoples of the third millennium lived in large houses that could contain a clan, rather than a nuclear family. Based on the evidence of paleolithic burials, there were no status differences between the sexes.

From this very early phase of civilization in which small bands of persons, a communal kin group, lived relatively autonomously, society became organized into larger units and divided into class hierarchies. Reasons for these changes must remain conjectural, but several theories have been proposed. One influential theory, published by Friedrich Engels in *The Origin of the Family, Private Property and the State* (1884), traced the subjugation of women to an increase in barter or trade. Trading involves the accumulation of goods to be exchanged and leads to specialization of work and a loss of direct control over the goods produced. Engels believed that this process eventually caused an accumulation of wealth controlled by men and a subsequent division of society into economic classes. Engels' theories have come under criticism by most modern anthropologists because he failed to take into account other important factors, such as the organization of work, the types of social networks that link persons to power structures, or the ways in which food is acquired. All such aspects of a culture can influence the division of labor between the sexes.

Some contemporary anthropologists emphasize that in societies divided into socioeconomic classes, there is a clear distinction between the private, domestic realm—identified with women, and the public sphere—identified with men.[6] Such a division has characterized most cultures in Western civilization but would not be as

significant when societies are organized around kinship networks in which the family
unit is not isolated from the public activities of the tribe. Whether such distinctions
were important factors affecting sex roles and status in prehistoric cultures can never
be conclusively documented.

WOMEN OF CRETE

By the third millennium, B.C., the Minoan civilization on the island of Crete was a
matriarchal theocracy ruled by a queen-priestess. This culture demonstrated a relatively high status for women. Minoan women had access to all professions, including
the manufacture of their famous pottery, which was distributed throughout the ancient
world. It is therefore possible that the *Octopus Vase* (Figure 2), for example, was
made by a woman craftsperson. The numerous statuettes of snake goddesses depicting a bare-breasted woman holding snakes in each hand (Figure 3) document female

FIGURE 2. Octopus vase, from Palaikastro, Crete. c. 1500 B.C. H:
11″. Archaeological Museum, Heraklion, Crete. Courtesy Hirmer
Verlag München.

FIGURE 3. Snake Goddess, from the Palace at Knossos. c. 1600 B.C. H: 13½". Archaeological Museum, Heraklion, Crete. Courtesy Hirmer Verlag München.

participation as divinity and priestess in Minoan society. This relatively high status for women on Crete may be a holdover from the egalitarian communism of an earlier epoch. It is believed that the first settlers of Crete came originally from Anatolia, and their culture seems related to the earlier practices of the Anatolian tribes, such as the community of Çatal Hüyük.

WOMEN OF THE ANCIENT NEAR EAST

By contrast, in the emergent contemporary civilization of Sumer, the subordination of women was well under way by the third millennium, B.C. In this culture of the "fertile crescent" in the ancient Near East, political power became centralized in the hands of male military leaders and hierarchical class stratification of the society began. Women were excluded from decision making and became another form of private property. This process is documented by the marriage laws that controlled women's lives to a great extent. Marriages were arranged by parents. The groom paid a "bride's price" to the parents of the bride. After marriage the husband became undisputed head of the family. He could divorce his wife quite easily or sell or pawn her to pay off his debts. While husbands could maintain concubines, a wife's adultery became a crime punishable by death. Children, like wives, were considered property of economic value.[7]

There is no evidence for female infanticide in Mesopotamia because the more children a man possessed, the greater his economic worth became. Abortion was considered a serious crime, and the society encouraged numerous births. A woman who was a mother had higher status and better legal rights than a woman who was not.

Because the main occupation of most women was the bearing and raising of children, the education of daughters focused on instruction in household tasks, which included weaving, needlework, and music making. However, women were not totally excluded from the economy. Many women were literate and signed documents and contracts in their own names. They could buy and sell slaves and other forms of property. Women could act as witnesses in court. A few women were priestesses living in convents and conducting a wide variety of business affairs independently of men.

Lower-class women and female slaves were active in many types of jobs and contributed to the economic development of their societies in the ancient Near East. Women were scribes, midwives, singers, tavern-keepers, and even chemists (thirteenth century B.C.). Records from as early as the third millennium B.C. show that women were brewers, cooks, and agricultural workers, occupations associated with women into the eighteenth century, A.D..

As in Çatal Hüyük and Crete, women made pottery. A cylinder seal from the early third millennium B.C. shows women potters making vessels in what appears to be a workshop.[8] Basket plaiting was another craft practiced by women of all classes.

Women predominated in the making of textiles, a laborious and time-consuming activity that could be done in the home and was therefore well suited to women. The fibers of flax, cotton, or wool first had to be cleaned and prepared and spun into thread. Then the thread was woven into cloth. Clothing was often decorated with embroidery. All these tasks were the exclusive concern of women. Female slaves who were skilled weavers were highly valued and in great demand in the ancient Near East. The upper classes purchased fine garments, beautifully decorated. Such items were also economically valuable commodities for export.

The professional activities of women in the Near East were largely confined to women of the artisan and slave classes, who were forced to work for survival. In royal families, women were secluded in harems. Within the harem, women practiced spinning and weaving, as well as embroidery and basket plaiting. But aristocratic women (as in the Middle Ages) performed these tasks for the domestic needs of the household, not as professional skills.

WOMEN OF GREECE

The contribution of women to the culture of their society is dependent first and foremost on their survival to maturity. Archeological evidence indicates that the Greeks practiced female infanticide, and that males outnumbered females by at least two to one.[9] This smaller proportion of females surviving infancy extends from the Greek Dark Ages (1100–800 B.C.) through the Classical and Hellenistic periods. By the Hellenistic era (fourth to first centuries B.C.), even fewer children of either sex were raised.

A Greek girl who survived infancy was fed an inferior diet. Girls were married between the ages of twelve and fifteen; men were usually married at thirty. Such young marriages forced women into early pregnancies, further threatening their survival. The shortage of women plus selective rearing also ensured that women would have multiple pregnancies. Many women did not survive the childbearing years, and women's life expectancy was five to ten years shorter than men's. One may conclude that only a fraction of the female population lived long enough to practice any profession without being pregnant or responsible for the care of small children.

As in the ancient Near East, marriage and motherhood were the most widely accepted and expected roles for women to fill in the society. However, the position of wife and mother conferred varying status on women in different periods. The status of some royal women in the Bronze Age, as described in the Homeric epics (ca. 1200 B.C.) was very high, and evidence also indicates that women were dominant in the religious sphere.[10] By contrast, the status of Greek women in the culture of the Classical era (fifth century B.C.), especially in Athens, seems to have been very low, and this may be explained by a number of factors. Particularly among the upper classes, a sharp separation existed between the men's public world and the women's domestic one, a situation similar to that in modern capitalist cultures. While men were occupied with running the Athenian democracy and waging almost continual warfare, upper-class women rarely left their homes. They remained in segregated quarters, often on the upper story of town houses. While boys were taught the arts of rhetoric and other intellectual pursuits, girls learned domestic crafts from their mothers. The age discrepancy between husband and wife and the gaps between the education of men and women further intensified the isolation between the sexes in Classical Athens.[11]

Considering the severe restrictions on women's lives, their inability to move freely in society, conduct business, or acquire any type of non-domestic training, it is not surprising to find that no names of important artists have come down to us from the Classical era. Only the poet Sappho (ca. 600 B.C.) received high praise from the Greeks: Plato referred to her as the twelfth Muse. Significantly, she came not from Athens or Sparta but from Lesbos, an island whose culture incorporated a high regard for women.

Further evidence of the low status of women is that no statues of female nudes survive from the Classical period. This is consistent with the belief that only the male body could be appreciated as an object of beauty. When female figures were created in sculpture, they were always clothed. Female nudes began to appear in the fourth century, accompanied by a correspondingly improved status for women in the society at large.

The Athenian woman, daughter of a citizen, always had a dowry that was meant to remain intact when she married. The dowry provided her with some degree of economic security. In the absence of sons, a daughter could legally inherit the family wealth, but the nearest male relative was supposed to marry the heiress. While women could acquire property through their dowries or by inheritance or gift, they had no legal rights. Women could not conduct business or sign contracts for major sums. Furthermore, because few women were literate, it was virtually impossible for women to conduct a business enterprise independently of men.

Greek women of all classes were occupied with the same types of work, mostly centered around the domestic needs of the family. Women cared for young children, nursed the sick, and prepared food. Wealthy women supervised slaves who did these tasks. Poorer women who could not afford to remain at home worked for wages at these jobs. There is evidence that some lower-class women sold retail goods in the marketplace.

Throughout this period in the Greek world, one of the major tasks of women was the weaving of textiles and their decoration. Women of all classes contributed to the making of cloth. Wealthy women and slaves worked in their homes, while poorer women earned wages as wool workers in the cloth industry. Spindles used to spin flax or wool into thread have been found in graves from the Dark Ages, identifying these as burial places of females.

Many female figures, including Helen and Penelope, are occupied with spinning and weaving in the *Iliad* and the *Odyssey*. Penelope, the wife of Odysseus, spends her days weaving a shroud for her dead husband and her nights unraveling it to evade her suitors. This is her primary activity and can be taken as an example of the importance of weaving in the life of the Greek upper-class woman. In Athens, a robe (peplos) for the cult statue of the goddess Athena was woven every four years. Two young girls selected from among the noble families of Athens would spin the yarn for the cloth. Other women then assisted in the weaving and embroidering of this holy garment. The culmination of the Panathenaic procession was the presentation of the peplos to the statue of Athena on the Parthenon, as depicted in the Parthenon frieze. Representations on Greek vases of women spinning or weaving far outnumber the pictures of other crafts. For example, the black-figured painting on a lekythos (Figure 4) illustrates women occupied in a variety of tasks related to the making of cloth.

FIGURE 4. ATTRIBUTED TO THE AMASIS PAINTER. Lekythos. Women working wool on a loom. H.: 6 3/4''. Said to have been found in Attica. The Metropolitan Museum of Art, Fletcher Fund, 1931.

Textile manufacture was a primary occupation for women in other areas of the ancient world outside of Greece. As noted before, women of all classes in the ancient Near East made textiles. Phoenician women were famous for their fine cloths. In the excavations of Troy, many weaving tools have been found.

Women were not only responsible for the manufacture of cloth but also for its decoration. Embroidery was an exclusively female occupation in Greece. In the decoration of textiles, women were the tastemakers of antiquity. Here, they had an outlet for their visual creativity.

Kate McK. Elderkin has built a convincing case for the influence of textile patterns and decoration on the successive stylistic development of Greek pottery design.[12] She maintains that the geometric style, as seen in the Dipylon pottery vases of the eighth century B.C. (Figure 5), was derived from the ornamental patterns found in Dorian wool fabrics. Not only the specific forms, but also the use of bands, is consistent with the weaving of wool fabrics. Ornamentation in bands is a noteworthy characteristic of Corinthian ware, such as the famous François Vase. In the later Archaic period, i.e., the sixth century B.C., fashions changed and the less decorated linen chiton of the Ionians gained popularity. The painted decoration on pottery subsequently became less ornate and the influence of weaving became less pronounced in this epoch.

FIGURE 5. Dipylon Amphora (Geometric Style), from the Dipylon Cemetery, Athens. c. 750 B.C. H.: 61″. National Archaeological Museum, Athens. Courtesy Hirmer Verlag München.

Athena was the patron goddess of both weavers and potters, connecting both of these activities with women, although by the Classical era it was mostly men who made pottery. Some women did continue to practice this craft. A woman is shown decorating a vase on a Greek red-figured hydria from the fifth century B.C. She is depicted in a workshop setting.

During the Hellenistic era (fourth to first centuries B.C.), Greek women received a rudimentary education, learning to read and write (except in Athens). In exceptional cases, women could study with a philosopher. By the fourth century B.C., the women of Sparta controlled two-fifths of the land through dowries and inheritance. Since much of the male population was away at war, the Spartan women enjoyed substantial freedom.

An increased status and prestige, at least for royal and upper-class women, can be observed during the Hellenistic era:

> . . . many women wielded power as wives or mothers especially of weak kings and as regents for young sons or absent husbands. . . the competent women visible in Hellenistic courts were one of the positive influences of this period toward increasing the prestige of non-royal but upper-class women.[13]

During this period there were more public decrees honoring the activities of women, a few women even held public office, and nude statues of goddesses proliferated.

While very few artists' names of either sex survive from antiquity, the earliest recorded names of women painters are found in Hellenistic texts. Unfortunately, none of the works of these artists have survived. In 228 B.C., Nealkes of Sicyon had his daughter trained as a painter.[14] Another Greek painter known by name alone was Eirene, daughter of Kratinos, who was famous for a painting in the city of Eleusis. Eirene is singled out for special mention in Boccaccio's *Concerning Famous Women*.[15] Boccaccio's treatise, largely dependent on the Roman historian Pliny, is a very important Renaissance source, preserving for his era the names of notable women of antiquity. Boccaccio also mentions Thamyris, or Timarete. This artist's reputation was based on a painting of the goddess Diana, guarded at the sanctuary in Ephesus. It is, of course, possible that women were painters in earlier periods and that their names, like those of their male colleagues, have simply been lost in history. To my knowledge, no evidence of women sculptors or architects in the ancient world has survived.

Long before the appearance of women painters in literary records, women had been credited in legend with the invention of this art. In both Eastern and Western cultures, the origin of the art of painting is attributed to the observation of a shadow and the tracing of that outline. By the time Pliny recorded the legend, the inventor of painting was identified as a woman, i.e., the "Corinthian Maid." The Maid traced her lover's profile on a wall. Subsequently, her father, the potter Butades, built up the work into a sculpture. The Corinthian Maid is often called "Dibutade," i.e., the daughter of Butades. A variation of this legend is recorded by Athenagoras, a Christian Athenian of the second century A.D. The first artist is now called "Core."

The legend of the Corinthian Maid was first widely used as a subject for the visual arts during the era of romantic classicism, in the late eighteenth century A.D. One art historian, Robert Rosenblum, believes that the increased popularity of the story of Dibutade at that time is related to the prominence of contemporary artists such as Angelica Kauffman and Elisabeth Vigée-Lebrun.[16] The careers of these artists will be discussed in chapters six and seven.

The legend of Dibutade and the preservation of the names of these women painters from the past have immense importance for the history of women artists. Despite their limited number, these notable painters served as role models for women artists from the Renaissance through the nineteenth century. Eirene, Timarete, and the other women recorded by Pliny and included in Boccaccio's study were incorporated into many subsequent histories of women artists.[17] Even though their works are lost, their reputations remained alive, preserving the idea that women could become excellent painters.

WOMEN OF ROME

The process of increasing freedom and status for upper-class women, begun in the Hellenistic era, continued into Roman times. Groups of women, such as the Sabines, played an important role in the early history of the Roman Republic. The famous Cornelia, who lived in the second century B.C., was considered a paragon of virtues: "She possessed an excellent Greek education, was a master of rhetoric such as no other woman was and corresponded with philosophers, scientists and distinguished men of affairs."[18] Through her sons, the Gracchi (their father was the tribune Tiberius Sempronius Gracchus), she exerted political influence as well. Cornelia was a model figure not only for subsequent generations of Roman matrons but also for later centuries. (See Kauffman's *Cornelia, Mother of Gracchi*, Figure 34.) As in Sparta, the prolonged absence of men on military campaigns and the administration of a far-flung empire gave upper-class women greater autonomy.

Nevertheless, marriage and motherhood continued to be the main occupation of Roman matrons. The exposure of girl infants and early death in childbearing resulted in fewer women than men in Roman society.[19] During both the Republican era and the Empire, virtually all upper-class women were married. In fact, Augustus made marriage almost compulsory. Girls were married early, between the ages of twelve and fifteen. Motherhood conveyed great status, as well as economic benefits, on women. Unmarried women forfeited their inheritances and childless women lost half of their inheritances.

While the Roman matron acquired a measure of respect and power inside the home as *mater familias*, the *pater familias*, i.e., the father of the family, retained total control over the female members of his family. He had the literal power of life and death over his daughters and decided on their marriage partners. Legally, women could not control any money or transact business on their own, but in practice women did control and bequeath their wealth. The growing bureaucracy of the Empire served to protect the rights of wives and children. A wife's dowry had to be returned intact if her husband repudiated the marriage.

> The growing custom of marriage *sine manu* enabled a women to remain under the power of her own family rather than being transferred to her husband's on the simple condition that she live for three days of every year in her father's house. By the beginning of the third century, [the Roman jurist] Ulpian said that a woman had to have a tutor to act for her at law, to make contracts, to emancipate slaves or to undertake civil business. But he added that a woman who had borne three children was no longer subject to this regula-

tion. Thus, the Roman woman, entirely powerless within the public structure, could exercise very considerable power in private life as a result of the wealth and property that she might accumulate by herself or through her family.[20]

Upper-class girls were educated by private tutors, but the early age of marriage limited the extent of their education. However, as was also true of the Renaissance, education and other accomplishments were considered positive attributes for women. Because women were not so completely isolated from male company as in Classical Athens, a woman was expected to be able to converse intelligently with men. Large numbers of upper-class women were interested in literature and a few were even authors and poets. Numerous orations honoring women have survived, indicating a public approval of notable women.

Spinning and weaving continued to be a major preoccupation of women of all classes:

> The old-fashioned Roman bride wreathed the doorposts of her new home with wool. When Augustus wished to instill respect for old-fasioned virtues among the sophisticated women of his household, he set them to work in wool and wore their homespun results. Many women of the lower classes, slave and freed, were also employed in working wool both at home and in small-scale industrial establishments where working-class men joined women as weavers and weighers of balls of wool to be apportioned to weavers. Spinning, however, continued to be solely women's work.[21]

Lower-class women practiced a number of occupations. In Pompeii, there were women physicians and "commercial entrepreneurs," as well as prostitutes, waitresses, and tradeswomen. Slaves worked as domestics and, as noted above, in the clothing industry. "Freed women and female slaves worked as fishmongers, barley-sellers, silk weavers, lime burners, clothes-menders . . . as midwives and nurses . . . stenographers, singers, and actresses, among other professions."[22]

Iaia of Kyzikos is the only name of a Roman woman artist that has been preserved. According to Pliny, "She painted chiefly portraits of women. . . . No artist worked more rapidly than she did, and her pictures has such merit that they sold for higher prices than those of Sopolis and Dionysios, well-known contemporary painters. . . ."[23]

Considering the wide variety of occupations practiced by Roman women, there may well have been other women painters whose names have not come down through the centuries. At any rate, the fact that Pliny recorded for posterity the names of a handful of women painters is a mark of the increased respect the Romans had for women of talent.

chapter 2

The Medieval World

During the long period known as the Middle Ages, women in different socioeconomic classes occupied a wide variety of roles and positions within their diverse cultures. For about a thousand years, from the collapse of the Roman Empire to the beginning of the Renaissance, society moved through a series of political and economic changes that affected the lives of women and the potential for them to act in the world. From the increased number of surviving documents, compared with the ancient world, the clearest picture emerges for women of the upper classes, the land-owning nobility. However, the general tendency, as the Middle Ages progressed, "was toward a lessening of the public activity of women, a lower place in ecclesiastical opinion, fewer roles in guild organizations, and less agricultural administration, if not less agricultural labor."[1]

Most of the works of art that have survived from the Middle Ages are related to the needs of the Church or the religious requirements of the nobility. Whether active in the construction and decoration of churches, the fabrication of magnificent sacramental objects in precious metals, the embroidering of clerical vestments, or the illumination of religious texts, the medieval artist/artisan, male or female, worked most often in anonymity. Where so few male artists are known by name, it is not surprising that the names of only a handful of women artists have survived from this epoch. Nothing, of course, precludes the possibility that more women artists of talent existed but did not sign their works and therefore remain unknown to modern scholars.

Throughout the Middle Ages, it would appear that large families were fairly common. The infant mortality rate remained high and many women died in childbirth. There is no evidence of infanticide. Earliest statistics, which date from the Carolingian era (ninth century), show that there were fewer adult females than males. This was the result of women's vulnerability to violence, mortality in childbirth, and lives of hard labor. However, after the thirteenth century, life expectancy was longer for women than for men. Furthermore, during the late Middle Ages, when reliable population statistics are available, there was a surplus of women. We know, for example, that in Bologna in the late fourteenth century, women formed a majority of the population over age 15. While many men were killed during the incessant warfare of the epoch, women in cities were protected from attack. Men also died in greater numbers during the plagues that repeatedly decimated the population. In addition to these natural causes for high male mortality, many more men than women took vows of celibacy as monks or clergy. Therefore, a certain proportion of the female population could not find mates. Among the upper classes, unmarried women were sent to convents. Women of the lower classes were always needed as workers, either in the urban shops of their fathers and brothers or as agricultural workers on rural manors.

During the Middle Ages, the situation of women was so intertwined with their class status that it is impossible to make any accurate generalizations about medieval women that cut across class lines. For that reason, the options of the women of the peasantry, the landed nobility, and the craft or artisan class in the towns will be discussed separately.

WOMEN PEASANTS

The largest number of women throughout this epoch belonged to the peasant class living on rural manors. Peasant women were involved in all activities of the manor except plowing. Their major responsibility was the production, preparation, and serving of food. They cooked, ran the dairy, cultivated the gardens, and tended poultry, in addition to performing many agricultural tasks. While aristocratic and upper-middle-class women were often literate, most lower-class women living on manors could not read or write. A peasant woman had practically no legal rights. She was dependent not only on her husband but also on the feudal lord. An old custom known as *ius primae noctis* or *droit du seigneur* entitled the feudal lord to spend the first night with every bride on his land. This right was not always exercised in practice, but it remained for centuries a symbol of the lord's possession of the women of his manor. In Germany, a woman of the lower classes could dispose of only very small sums of money, and her husband had sole rights to the dowry.

WOMEN OF THE LANDED NOBILITY

During the early Middle Ages, women were often permitted to inherit land, usually in the absence of a male heir. In an epoch when all wealth was determined by the ownership of land, this gave a select group of women great power within their society. Beginning in the sixth century, daughters could inherit property, and the laws restricting inheritance rights of women were continually eased. By the mid-eighth century, both legally and in practice, women were often inheriting control over land. In the early

Middle Ages, with the exception of the Carolingian period in the ninth century when a centralized government under Charlemagne was established, women often wielded considerable political power through their ownership of property: While the Carolingian system deprived some women of their political influence, it eventually strengthened the position of secular women within the family. Marriage became indissoluble, and this protected women from capricious husbands and ensured their inheritance rights. Following the dissolution of the Carolingian empire, women of these classes benefited directly from the almost unlimited power of the family:

> Since land had become the only source of power, by exercising their property rights. . .a growing number of women appear in the tenth and eleventh centuries as. . .mistresses of landed property and castles with attendant rights of justice and military command, proprietors of churches and participants in both secular and ecclesiastical assemblies.[2]

Because a woman was allowed to bequeath her property as she wished, her position of power was consolidated. Women appear to be most important as landowners and managers when men are absent for extended periods during the frequent wars or the Crusades. By the early twelfth century, Eleanor of Aquitaine controlled a large portion of the lands of southern France, making her the most outstanding and famous example of a powerful female landowner. But there were others, especially in southern France and Spain where women were very prominent as landowners.

During the Middle Ages, marriage continued to be largely a financial and political arrangement. This was especially true in cases of heiresses. Often, women were betrothed and even married while still children. Once a woman was married, her legal rights were restricted. Wives were supposed to be obedient to their husbands. The husband, in turn, functioned as his wife's "guardian" and had to represent his wife in court. Only in the later Middle Ages could women act as witnesses in court. A widow, however, was permitted to act more independently than a wife or daughter. Many widows were named as executrixes in their husband's wills and thereby profited financially from their marriage contracts.

The wife of a nobleman living on a feudal estate was responsible for the smooth running of a large and complex household. Medieval manors were economically self-sufficient; virtually all the necessities of life had to be raised or made on the premises. The noblewoman supervised food preparation and production on the farm and dairy. Some of the cloth used for the household was produced at home, but in the later Middle Ages the expanding cloth industry of the towns provided textiles more cheaply than they could be produced in the manor. When it was no longer necessary to manufacture cloth on the manors, noblewomen often occupied themselves with embroidery and tapestry production, the most luxurious forms of needlework.

Large families were common among the upper classes, but the responsibilities of motherhood were not as demanding as in later epochs. Infants were usually turned over to wet nurses. Boys and girls left home at an early age to pursue their educations, and marriage took place at a very early age.

Girls born into noble families were provided with an education that could prepare them for the complex responsibilities of their existence. Some girls were sent to school in nunneries. Here, they learned to read, received religious instruction, and were taught the techniques of spinning and needlework. Sometimes, girls were also taught how to write and illuminate manuscripts. In addition to this type of education, girls were sent to the courts of great ladies where they could develop manners appropriate to their class. A certain level of intellectual attainment was acceptable for women of this class. They were often expected to be able to sing and to play a musical instrument.

When the lord and husband was in residence, the noblewoman's tasks focused on the domestic management of the estate in her roles as wife and mother. However, when the husband was absent, as was frequently the case during the Crusades and other military expeditions, the duties of the wife expanded dramatically. The medieval lady then took over all aspects of the management of the estate, even defending it from attack if necessary. If the lord was captured, she raised the money for his ransom. In his absence she was his sole representative for all necessary affairs.

The dominant role played by the noblewoman on her estate during her husband's absence is consistent with the activities of some queens who served as regents when their husbands, i.e., the kings, were not in residence at court. For example, Eleanor of Aquitaine was designated regent for Henry II and Matilda was regent for William the Conqueror.

Although not acting specifically as regent, some medieval queens were quite influential. The Carolingian queens of the ninth century were responsible for the distribution of funds from the royal treasury for the salaries of knights. It is likely that the queen also controlled the workshops on the manors, which supplied the funds that she dispensed. The wives of the three Ottonian Emperors in the tenth century used their influence to found convents which, through schools and in other ways, strengthened the dynasty of the emperors.

Not to be overlooked for the history of art, many queens and noblewomen were very active patrons of the arts, commissioning precious objects, books, goldsmith work, embroideries, and so on.

With a few notable exceptions, beginning in the mid-eleventh century the growth of cities and the increasing powers of the Church tended to restrict the wide range of roles that upper-class women had played in the tenth and early eleventh centuries. Compared with the early Middle Ages, women in the twelfth, thirteenth, and fourteenth centuries could not exercise the same range of power. Professional men took over the administration of their families' estates.

Furthermore, the custom of providing women with a dowry upon marriage rather than a portion of the family's land holdings was becoming more widespread. While this practice prevented the division of a family's property, thus improving the aristocracy's ability to withstand the growing power of the kings, it restricted the economic scope of women, which was largely based on control of land.

Courtly Love and Christian Dogma

As women's real power to act in the world diminished, a new art form developed in which women played a major role, i.e., the poetry of courtly love. Women of the courts, particularly in southern France, patronized the troubadours who sustained this movement. In this romantic cult, the noblewoman, as object of the poet's love, is worshipped almost as devoutly as the Virgin Mary in Christianity. "In chivalry, the romantic worship of a woman is as necessary a quality of the perfect knight as the worship of God."[3] Courtly love, by definition, was extramarital, and it was defined in physical terms. This glorification of the aristocratic lady, the object of the poet's romantic fantasies, is an artistic and intellectual construction that tells us little about the actual roles and contributions of these women to their society.

The romantic adoration of the noblewoman in the poetry of courtly love is one intellectual position diametrically opposed by the misogyny of Catholic religious teachings. From the time of the earliest church fathers, particularly St. Paul, Christian dogma viewed women as embodiments of evil. The ideal Christian life was spent in monastic isolation, avoiding pernicious contact with women. Women were tools of the devil, a bitter necessity for the continuation of the species. And because the clergy who avoided contact with women were the main portion of the population who were educated, their ideas received wide dissemination. St. Thomas Aquinas did not include women in his moral system. He wrote of "making use of a necessary object, woman, who is needed to preserve the species or to provide food and drink. . .woman was created to be man's helpmate, but her unique role is in conception. . .since for other purposes men would be better assisted by other men."[4]

It is an interesting contradiction that this fear and degradation of women coexisted with the Christian cult adoration of the Virgin Mary. The worship of Mary was a very widespread religious phenomenon in the later Middle Ages.

Nunneries

In addition to the role of lady of the manor, women of the upper classes could also become nuns. This was only possible for women of wealth because a dowry was required before a woman was permitted to join a convent. Furthermore, unmarried women of the lower classes were economically productive, and their labor was useful for the family unit. The nunneries provided a socially acceptable refuge for women whose only other alternative was marriage. The convent schools trained boys and girls of the upper classes. Convents also served as boarding houses for wealthy wives and widows who, for whatever reason, could no longer reside in their castles. Even though the contemplative life of a nun was an available option for only a small percentage of the female population, nunneries fulfilled an important purpose for upper-class women. Freed from male domination, some women could exercise leadership skills, powers of organization, and management of a complex estate. Especially in the early Middle Ages, between 500 and 700 A.D., nunneries not only preserved learning and maintained culture but often exercised power through their land holdings. The power of abbesses, rivaled only by queens, was equal to that of abbotts and even bishops.

Nunneries permitted women to pursue lives dedicated to spiritual contemplation, which was highly respected in the society of the Middle Ages, so dominated by religious concerns. Furthermore, convents provided a good education for the nuns and daughters of the nobility, although standards of education and literacy varied. The most learned women of the Middle Ages, those who made significant contributions to their culture, were nuns. As we will see, the convent scriptoria provided women with the opportunity to become artists.

St. Hildegarde of Bingen was the abbess of a convent in Germany. She is generally regarded as one of the greatest mystics of the Middle Ages. From her position as head of a convent she became quite famous in her epoch and corresponded with the most noted contemporary religious and political figures. Although not a painter herself, St. Hildegarde was believed to be responsible for the innovative design of the imagery that illustrated her visions, the *Scivias*. Although no surviving manuscript may be attributed to her hand, it is likely that her imagination, which extended to the invention of 950 words, also contributed to the form of the illustrations.

Herrad of Landsberg, Abbess of Hohenburg, is the author of a very important medieval pictorial encyclopedia, the *Hortus Delicarum*. The manuscript is known only through traced drawings made in the nineteenth century. These 636 miniatures document her strong visual imagination and earn her an imposing place in medieval art.

At the peak of their population, in 1250 A.D., there were 500 convents in Germany. By this time, however, the convent was no longer exercising a leadership role in the society, as in the early Middle Ages. Beginning in the mid-eleventh century, Church leadership was moving from the monastic system to the hierarchical political structure of the bishoprics and the papacy. Along with this development, the intellectual centers of the society shifted from the monasteries to the universities, where women were excluded.

Furthermore, the nunneries, suffering from insufficient endowment and bad management, were by the late Middle Ages in a noted state of decline. Latin was no longer widely understood, standards of education had fallen, and an increasing worldliness had penetrated the cloistered walls. Artists practicing within the convent were no longer exposed to changing stylistic developments, and the art produced was stylistically out of date by the beginning of the Renaissance. This decline may be attributed, at least in part, to the misogyny of the Catholic Church, which fostered a highly mixed attitude toward pious women who wished to pursue a contemplative life.

After the Gregorian reform movement of the late eleventh century, the formerly widespread practice of the double monastery, one for men and one for women, was abolished. Convents were thus excluded from the institutional hierarchy of the Church. There was no female monastic order, despite the efforts of a few men, most notably Pope Innocent III, who wished to keep the women's religious movement within the Church organization. The existing orders, such as the Franciscans, Dominicans, and Cistercians, were not receptive to the integration of nuns into their administrative domain. It is not surprising, given this unwillingness on the part of the established Church hierarchy to accept the administration of pious women, that women formed independent, semi-religious, unofficial communities. Beginning in the twelfth century, pious women known as Beguines gathered together to live in chastity and poverty. Most of these women were from the upper classes, both married and single, who renounced all worldly goods to pursue a penitential life and perform charitable acts.[5]

Significant numbers of women were also attracted to heretical sects that provided a wider role for women in their orders. The Waldensians and Carthars, for example, permitted women to preach and act as priests. The Albigensians also concerned themselves more directly with the position of women in society.

Medieval Manuscript Illuminators

Prior to the end of the thirteenth century, the production and illumination of sacred books was solely confined to monasteries and convents. For the history of art, this is the most important role of these institutions. The nunnery was the only place in that society where women could be trained as painters. Consequently, women painters of the Middle Ages came from the upper classes. A limited number of women manuscript illuminators who were nuns are known from the tenth to the sixteenth centuries. The attribution of a manuscript illumination to a woman can be authenticated only by a signature or self-portrait, and many medieval artists did not sign their works. It is possible that many even more important women artists are simply unnamed and therefore unknown.

The first major convent scriptoria, or book-making workshops, coincided with the revived interest in manuscript creation and preservation under the reign of Charlemagne. Charlemagne's sister Gisela directed the first Carolingian convent scriptorium at Chelles, northeast of Paris. Although one cannot firmly attribute a set of illuminations to women painters at the Chelles convent (which was part of a double institution of monastery and convent), other related manuscripts are signed by women. Also, there are literary references to illuminators who were nuns in England and Flanders in the eighth and ninth centuries.

The earliest manuscript firmly attributed to a woman is the Gerona Apocalypse, signed ''En depintrix'' and produced in Spain around 975. These paintings are very fine illustrations of the apocalypse compiled by Beatus. In the double-page painting reproduced here (Figure 6), one can see a strong sense of abstract design and linear energy. The horizontal registers provide both a base line for some figures and a background for other forms. The active curvilinear shape of the dragon and the drawing of the figures demonstrates a highly competent draftsmanship. Dorothy Miner has noted ''the sensitive play of sharp colors against disarmingly delicate ones. . .'' as another interesting and original element of En's style.[6] Furthermore, within the tradition of Mozarabic manuscript illuminations, the ''longer and more active bodies, pale complexions and. . .lively silhouettes''[7] of the figures are personal stylistic elements of this talented and innovative artist.

The numerous German nunneries mentioned earlier account for the fact that most known female manuscript illuminators of the Middle Ages were German nuns. A self-portrait identifies Claricia as the illuminator of a manuscript made in Augsburg, Germany in the twelfth century. In a clever way, Claricia painted herself swinging from the body of the initial ''Q.'' Another illuminator named Guda inserted her

FIGURE 6.   EN. *Battle of the Dragon with Child of the Women.* Beatus Apocalypse. Gerona Cathedral, Gerona, Spain.

own image in a manuscript from Frankfurt also dating from the twelfth century. While Guda is in a nun's habit, Claricia appears in ordinary clothes. Claricia might have been an upper-class woman who was sent to a convent for schooling—a common practice. "It becomes clearer and clearer as the Middle Ages move on that miniature painting was regarded as an appropriate occupation and a becoming accomplishment for a lady."[8] The future recommendation of Castiglione in the sixteenth century, advising women of the courts to acquire painting skills, is merely a continuation of a widespread practice in the Middle Ages and not the initiation of a new set of expectations for women of the upper classes.

In Dominican convents in southern Germany in the late fourteenth and early fifteenth centuries, a large number of women were trained as manuscript illuminators. By this time, however, with the developments of the Renaissance, convents were too isolated to keep pace with the changes of style in the art produced in the secular world.

URBAN WORKING WOMEN

With the emergence of towns and cities toward the end of the Middle Ages, women took on some new roles and continued some old ones in the urban economy. Girls in the later Middle Ages had a slightly better chance of receiving a rudimentary education in the towns than in the countryside. In 1272, there was one public elementary school for girls in Paris, but eleven such schools for boys. All women of the lower classes contributed in some way to the economic stability of their family unit. Girls, like boys, were often apprenticed to learn a trade. The female apprentice was under the direct supervision of the master's wife. Wives and daughters most often worked in the family's commercial enterprise. Many wives, not directly active in their husband's trade, would handle the retail end of the business. Because there was a surplus of women, unmarried women were forced to support themselves and often worked for wages or ran their own businesses. "Under English common law, the unmarried woman or widow, the *femme sole*—was, as far as all private, as distinct from public rights and duties are concerned, on a par with men."[9] In certain cases when women were conducting businesses of their own, even a married woman could be treated as a *femme sole* in England.

A number of women workers were employed in the manufacture and sale of food and beverages. The bread-making and brewing industries were dominated by women. Women often sold food in markets and were innkeepers. These types of employment continued the traditional identification of women with food preparation for the family.

Of greatest interest for the history of art is the wide range of craft and artisan activities practiced by women in medieval towns. In Paris by the late thirteenth century, women were working at 108 occupations of the most diverse kinds. Women were shoemakers, tailors, barbers, jewelers, goldsmiths, bookbinders, painters, and many other skilled artisans. Of the 110 craft guilds that existed in Paris, five restricted membership to women only.

Another important female occupation during the Middle Ages and continuing into the seventeenth century was midwifery. However, while midwives could practice family medicine and obstetrics, they were not permitted to become professional physicians.[10]

A large number of women were occupied in the rapidly expanding textile industry. In fact, the making of wool, linen, and silk cloths was one of the major occupations of women until the eighteenth century and the Industrial Revolution. Women performed nearly all the work in the preliminary processes of cloth making—combing and carding the fibers, spinning the yarn, etc. Women holding distaff and spindle, the tools of the trade, appear frequently in the marginalia of medieval manuscripts. In England, the Netherlands, northern France, and Italy many women worked at these tasks. The term "spinster," i.e., one who spins, originally identified a person's occupation. By the seventeenth century, the term had acquired the additional meaning of "an unmarried woman," indicating the virtually total identification of spinning with women. Weaving was also a female occupation in the thirteenth century, but by the sixteenth century this craft was taken over by the all male weavers' guilds.

In addition to the wool trades, women dominated the silk-making industry in France. The women who spun the thread and made the silk cloth were paid notoriously low wages. The manufacture of silk belts and alms purses was the responsibility of women's guilds. Until the fourteenth century, dressmaking and embroidery were also female-dominated activities. In fact, English women embroiderers perfected this art in the thirteenth century. Their creations are collectively known as *opus*

Anglicanum. These embroidered church vestments and garments were highly desired by the nobility and clergy all over Europe.

While women were very active in a wide range of crafts throughout the Middle Ages, their relationship to the guilds varied widely. Guilds were powerful trade organizations that limited membership in the professions and established regulations controlling the products.

In Paris, women could become independent members of a guild as early as the thirteenth century and were subject to the same regulations as men. Crafts monopolized by women were organized in the same way as crafts with greater male participation.

In the fourteenth century women were often members of German guilds. However, by the fifteenth century, during the Renaissance, women began to be excluded more and more from membership in Italian and German guilds. It would seem that fear of competition from women who worked at lower wages was the main rationale for their exclusion. The male guild members did not want to be undercut by cheaper female labor.

In England women were almost never admitted as full members to a guild, and there were no guilds for the female-dominated industries. Exceptions were made for widows, who were regularly admitted as full members of their husbands' guilds. Many widows carried on their husbands' businesses, documenting their active partnership in the trade. The progressive exclusion of women from full membership in professional organizations continued into the sixteenth century. "By 1600 women had disappeared almost completely from professional life."[11]

Secular Manuscript Illuminators

In northern Europe, unlike Italy, the art of illuminating manuscripts did not occupy a secondary place to large-scale fresco painting. This form of painting was highly valued and actively supported by the leading art patrons of the era.

As early as the thirteenth century, commercial book illustrators, as opposed to monks and nuns, ran businesses in the cities of Europe. While never very numerous, women painters and sculptors did exist by the late thirteenth and early fourteenth centuries, as documented by tax records. Etienne Boileau's *Livre des Métiers* (1270) refers to a guild of female book illuminators and binders.[12] Women artists were usually members of a family of male artists. As noted earlier, in the artisan classes women regularly worked in the family business.

In 1405 an important feminist writer, Christine de Pisan, wrote a defense of her sex entitled *The City of Women.* Inspired by Bocaccio's *Concerning Famous Women,* which had been translated into French in 1402, Christine de Pisan enumerates the merits of women. In this text, she praises the illuminations of a contemporary artist, Anastaise:

> . . .with regard to painting at the present time I know a woman called Anastaise, who is
> so skillful and experienced in painting the borders of manuscripts and the backgrounds
> of miniatures that no one can cite a craftsman in the city of Paris, the center of the best il-

luminators on earth, who in these endeavors surpasses her in any way. . . .And this I know by my own experience, for she has produced some things for me which are held to be outstanding among the ornamental borders of the great masters.[13]

It would seem that Anastaise specialized in the less prestigious aspects of manuscript painting, i.e., backgrounds and borders. Yet her skills were clearly impressive enough for Christine de Pisan to extol, thereby leaving a record of her existence for posterity.

Although not mentioned in *The City of Women,* at about the same point in history another woman artist, Bourgot, was actively employed by the most important patrons of her era in the decoration of manuscripts. Bourgot was the daughter of the painter Jean Le Noir.[14] Le Noir and Bourgot executed a Book of Hours for Yolande de Flandres, an important and active patron of the era around 1353. This "delicious and delicate" manuscript continued the inventive traditions of Jean Pucelle, but "infused it with a more sturdy expressionism."[15] They moved to Paris where they worked for the King of France, Charles V. Le Noir received payments from Jean, Duc de Berry in 1372 and 1375. The list of their sophisticated patrons testifies to the skills and reputations of Le Noir and Bourgot. Although it is difficult to distinguish the creative contribution of Bourgot from that of her father, one may assume that she was at least a highly competent craftsperson, if not the creative force of the team.

By the fifteenth century, women would appear to be even more active in the art of book painting. The records of the painters' guild in Bruges, which admitted women as members, reveal that 12 percent of the guild members were female in 1454, and that the proportion had increased to 25 percent by the 1480s. As Harris suggests, such extensive participation in this field is an essential background for the emergence of Flemish miniature painters in the sixteenth century.

From this account it is clear that both in convents and commercial enterprises, women formed a small but not insignificant percentage of the artists active as manuscript illuminators. While it is impossible to identify the precise contributions of these craftswomen, their existence can be either inferred from general custom in the society or documented when guild records included women and have been studied by modern historians.

Medieval Embroidery

The association between women and the decoration of textiles with embroidery can be traced back to the ancient world. This time-consuming activity is usually associated with women of the upper classes who had the leisure to devote to the art. During the Middle Ages, many women were taught to embroider, and they used this skill to fashion some of the most significant but fragile works of their epoch. In many of the homes of noblewomen, embroidery was not a casual pastime but a serious occupation, an organized domestic activity.

Embroidery is not widely considered a "fine art" today. In fact, it ranks fairly low on the hierarchical scale of the crafts. In the Middle Ages, however, embroidery was widely appreciated as an art form. The most noted historian of medieval English embroidery has characterized the status of this medium in the following way: "A vast quantity of work never since equalled in design, technique, or quality of materials employed was produced throughout Europe. In England the art of needlework attained such notable perfection that its masterpieces challenged comparison with the finest paintings."[16] When the status of the art of embroidery is this high, the largely anonymous creators of these works rank with the leading artists of their era.

In the early Middle Ages, prior to the development of the town economies of the twelfth and thirteenth centuries, embroidery was made in convents and in the homes of noblewomen. In Carolingian convents, teams of women produced fine fabrics used for vestments or as export commodities to be sent to Byzantium in exchange for gold. Women's work thus produced one of the few marketable export items of the economy.

Many convents were occupied with the creation of elaborate embroideries used for priests' vestments or as an offering to a saint. These objects were frequently encrusted with pearls and other jewels and often sewn with gold and silver thread. The earliest reference to a woman embroiderer is St. Etheldreda, Abbess of Ely, who lived in the seventh century. She "offered to St. Cuthbert a stole and maniple, a fine and magnificent embroidery of gold and precious stones, worked, it is said, with her own hands, for she was a skillful craftswoman in gold embroidery."[17]

Convent schools taught the arts of needlework to the daughters of the landed nobility as part of their premarital education. This factor, combined with the transmission of techniques informally from generation to generation, not merely preserved the art but helped to stimulate its practice. Noblewomen prided themselves on the skill of their needlework, lavished on clothing as well as on the decoration of church vestments. The stole and maniple worked by order of Queen Aelfflaed, wife of Edward the Elder (ca. 910) have been preserved in Durham Cathedral. The work demonstrates the extreme finesse and technical excellence of the art of embroidery at this time.

In addition to the use of embroidery to decorate religious garments, we know of at least one tapestry that illustrated a narrative of the deeds of a nobleman. Around 991, a woman named Aedelfleda presented the church at Ely with a hanging embroidery illustrating the achievements of her husband. This work, although now lost, may have inspired Odo, Bishop of Bayeux, to commission the most famous embroidered work of the Middle Ages, the Bayeux Tapestry.

The Bayeux Tapestry is a unique surviving masterpiece of the medieval art of needlework.[18] Made around 1070, it depicts events surrounding the invasion of England by William the Conqueror in the year 1066. The narrative is a moral tale of the downfall of Harold who broke his oath, sworn at Bayeux. Whether the historical account of the Norman Conquest documented in the Bayeux Tapestry should be considered reliable history is less important than the fact that the tapestry was almost certainly executed by teams of women, following the cartoons of a single designer of undetermined sex. Worked in brightly dyed wool on linen, the Bayeux Tapestry is 230 feet long. The elaborate detail, lively movement of men and animals, and sophisticated composition prove that it is a work of highest quality.

The energy and activity of the narrative in the Bayeux Tapestry is shown in this banquet scene (Figure 7). Roasted poultry on skewers is taken off the fires and placed on a sideboard. The horn informs the company that dinner is served. Bishop Odo, seated in the center of the semicircular table, says grace; William the Conqueror is seated at his right. The scene uses green, red, and yellow thread that retains some of its original brilliance. The precision of the needlework demonstrates the exceptional technical capabilities of the workers. The decorative borders, enlivened with composite animals, provide additonal scope for inventive designs.

Opus Anglicanum

As early as the eleventh century, some lower-class women earned their living practicing the art of embroidery. By 1250, professional women embroiderers in England had an international reputation and their creations were in great demand. The popes frequently ordered embroidered vestments from English workshops. Royalty, clerics, and wealthy persons all over Europe wanted to own examples of the now renowned *opus Anglicanum,* the term used to refer to works of embroidery created at this time in England. Around 1240, Mabel of Bury St. Edmonds "was possibly the foremost worker," according to Christie. In the early fourteenth century, Rose of Burford, wife of a London merchant, received a commission from Queen Isabella of Spain to decorate a vestment intended as a gift to the Pope.

After 1250, the demand for examples of *opus Anglicanum* was so great that there was a shift from production by individuals in scattered homes to an organized commercial activity in the towns. With this shift the names of more men appear in

FIGURE 7.   *Bayeux Tapestry.* Detail. c. 1073–1083. Wool embroidery on linen. H.: 20''. Town Hall, Bayeux, France.

connection with this art, although they may have been acting more as intermediaries. We do know that by the thirteenth century, a master craftsman such as a goldsmith was considered perfectly competent to supply a design for an embroidered vestment, although the actual fabrication of the garment may well have remained in the hands of women. At first, men may have restricted their role to supervision and management of female workers. "Modern scholars note a general decline in the quality of embroidery being produced by the fourteenth century but without commenting on the growing role of men in this hitherto female craft. By the fifteenth century, we hear of traveling teams of embroiderers, a situation incompatible with extensive female participation."[19] Whether one should attribute this diminished excellence to the greater participation of men or the changing methods of production remains undetermined.

Women artists in the Middle Ages were not among the major painters of fresco cycles, the architects of cathedrals, nor the foremost sculptors of their era. However, their talents did emerge, under the proper sociological conditions, in the media of needlework and manuscript illumination. Anonymous, like most of their male colleagues, these women artists, particularly the secular artists, form a backdrop of activity in the visual arts that was necessary for the emergence of specific women creators in the ensuing Renaissance period.

chapter 3

Introduction
to the Renaissance Era:
1400–1780

The political and economic reorganization of society that marks the shift from the Middle Ages to the Renaissance was a slow and complex process that occurred at different times in different parts of Europe. Beginning in Italy in the thirteenth century, an urban economy based on commerce and the accumulation of money began to replace the medieval system of feudalism in which power and wealth were measured by the ownership of land. This process was well underway by the fourteenth century in Italy and continued through the fifteenth and sixteenth centuries in the rest of Europe and England.

During the fifteenth century, women usually married at age 15 or 16. Beginning in the sixteenth century, women in southern Europe were married by age 20, but women in northern Europe did not marry until their mid-20s. By the eighteenth century, women in England and France did not marry until age 24 or 25. The postponement of marriage to a later age tended to reduce the overall number of pregnancies and to limit the size of families as compared with earlier epochs. By having fewer pregnancies and bearing children at a more physically mature age, the life expectancy for women was improved. But because both infant and maternal mortality rates remained quite high throughout the eighteenth century, population growth was slow.

The shift to delayed marriage left a sizable minority of unmarried women. Some of these women became the targets of the widespread witch trials of the sixteenth and seventeenth centuries. No part of Europe was immune from witchcraft trials. The largest number of trials and executions occurred under the Holy Roman Empire. "From 1480 to 1700 more women were killed for witchcraft than for other crimes put together."[1]

As in the Middle Ages, the class status of women was more critical than sex in determining a woman's options. It is necessary, therefore, to consider the diverse situations of women in various socioeconomic classes to understand the ways in which their options affected their potential to become professional artists.

34

PEASANTS AND LOWER-CLASS WOMEN

Among the lower classes and peasants in the rural areas of Europe, women were active contributors to the family economy throughout this period. Peasant women continued to work at the wide variety of tasks they had performed on the feudal manors. These included agricultural chores, care of farm animals, and dairy production.

In eighteenth-century preindustrial England and France, the majority of women worked in a household setting. Single women worked either for their families or outside for wages, depending on the specific needs of their parental family unit. A single woman also tried to accumulate a small amount of capital to help her set up her own household. Marriage was simply the establishment of a new family economy, the basic unit of reproduction and of work.

Since productivity was low and production was most often located in the home, the bearing of children did not seriously interrupt a woman's working potential. "Views of children and standards of child care were such that children were either sent away at a young age or were incorporated into adult routines and adult work."[2] Hence, a married woman could balance her responsibilities for running the household and bearing children with a home industry in which she could earn wages or create a product to be sold on the market. (Lace making was one such industry that employed large numbers of women in their homes.) Women were employed in "cottage industries" often as "spinsters" for low wages.

As we shall see, with the advent of the Industrial Revolution and the greater concentration of wage-earning potential outside the home, women encountered greater difficulties in balancing work for wages, maintenance of the household, and childbearing.

WOMEN OF THE UPPER CLASSES

The lives of women in the artisan and peasant classes were less dramatically transformed by the sociopolitical changes in society prior to the Industrial Revolution than were the lives of upper-class women. The scope of activities demanded and expected of the upper-class woman of the Renaissance was more narrowly restricted to the roles of wife and mother than it had been for the noblewoman under feudalism. "All the advances of Renaissance Italy, its proto-capitalist economy, its states, and its humanistic culture, worked to mold the noblewoman into an aesthetic object; decorous, chaste, and doubly dependent—on her husband as well as the prince."[3] The Florentine Renaissance design of the upper-class home, the *palazzo*, reflects this withdrawal of women from the public sphere and their confinement within the nuclear family. These spacious and private town houses substituted an enclosed courtyard for the earlier loggia that opened onto the street.

For most women of all classes, marriage and motherhood were expected roles. For upper-class women, the only other available option was the seclusion of the convent. Marriages were always arranged by parents and continued to be primarily an economic contract or an alliance between two families of the same class status. A daughter's chastity was an absolute necessity and a very high priority of the culture. Daughters were strictly supervised to ensure their virginity. Divorce was virtually unknown.

Women's legal rights throughout this era remained very limited. In general, husbands administered matters and made decisions. Women were not only excluded from holding public office, but also from participation in legal matters and law courts. For example, a law in Florence passed in 1415 forbade a married woman from drawing up her own will or disposing of her dowry to the detriment of her husband and children.[4] In Florence, women "could not adopt children, go bail for any body, act as guardian or representative of any person of minor age, except of their own children, and even for these they were not allowed to appoint a guardian."[5]

Almost all Renaissance treatises on women viewed them strictly as wives, regardless of class status. The most important virtue of the wife was obedience to the will of her husband. After obedience, chastity was an essential virtue. In a wife chastity signified sexual fidelity to her husband, and this was sometimes enforced by the "chastity belt." In addition, silence, discretion, love of her husband, and modesty are frequently cited as ideal qualities for the Renaissance woman. The gentle, passive aspects of her nature were extolled and cultivated; the more aggressive aspects of her character were repressed.

The list of virtues makes it clear that the upper-class woman in the Renaissance was subjugated emotionally to a greater extent than the noblewoman of the Middle Ages, who retained control over property and often ran the estate in the absence of her husband. One of the most important activities of the female members of the upper classes continued to be the spinning of wool and flax, although professional weavers organized in guilds actually made the cloth. Needlework was also deemed one of the most appropriate activities for women.

The education and training of the upper-class girl in the Renaissance was focused exclusively on her destined role of wife and the skills needed to maintain a household. Therefore, her education aimed primarily at

> . . .suppressing all individuality, fostering both fear of offense and complete dependence upon the will of her husband for all her comforts, and contentedness to live within the orbit of the house. . . .nothing must be allowed in the training of her mind that would encourage or enable her to compete on even ground with men. This general assumption is implicit in everything that was said on the training and education of women, in the limited aim set for their education even by their most ardent supporters, in the restriction on subjects and books, and most of all in the almost total absence of reference to the professions.[6]

While the Renaissance man received an education in a wide variety of subjects, Renaissance women were taught only those skills that would make them competent housewives, except for instruction in religious principles, which would encourage docility and obedience.

An exception to the limited level of education began to develop during the fifteenth century. The Humanists influenced the education of a small group of noblewomen, at first in the courts of Italy, then spreading through Europe. These ideals were incorporated into a "Christian Humanism" in England, France, and the Netherlands, spread by intellectuals like Erasmus and Thomas More. According to the Humanists, women should receive the same education as their male counterparts. Like the Renaissance man, women should study Latin, classical literature, philosophy, and history, as well as geometry, arithmetic, and astrology. This model was eventually adopted for the upper-class women of the towns as well as for the ladies at court. By the sixteenth century, under the influence of Humanism, schools for girls that taught minimal literacy were widespread in northern Europe.

These Humanist ideals also affected the training of artists. Artists were expected to possess a knowledge of science, mathematics, and perspective, as well as the practical skills acquired in an apprenticeship.

The noblewoman's education was affected by the publication of Castiglione's *The Courtier* in 1528. This book became an enormously influential treatise not only for the education of women but also for the definition of ideal modes of conduct for upper-class men and women. Castiglione grants to the noblewoman all the virtues and potential for perfection of the male courtier. Her education is equivalent to that of men. Most significantly for the history of art, all the arts practiced at court, i.e., music, writing, drawing, and painting, are seen as positive attributes for women.

These arts are not viewed as professional skills to be executed for money, but rather as appropriate accomplishments for a refined and properly educated noblewoman. Castiglione's ideas affected many women in the upper classes, the stratum of society from which some of the most important women artists of the sixteenth century, like Sofonisba Anguissola, emerge.

Another consequence of Castiglione's book was the perpetuation of the ideals of medieval courtly love, cast in a Neoplatonic context. This version of *courtoisie* survived into the Victorian era. One scholar sees this treatise as the source for the modern concept of the lady as a romantic object set on a pedestal.[7]

WOMEN AND THE REFORMATION

With the establishment of a married clergy in the Protestant religions, prevailing attitudes toward women became more positive. Marriage was viewed as a relationship based on "mutual aid, comfort and sustaining companionship."[8] Under Calvinism, women could take part in religious services as equals of men. Girls living in the towns of northern Europe learned to read and write, although their education rarely passed beyond minimal literacy. The Protestant girl also received instruction in religion and needlework. The Reformation continued to define women's realm in the strictly limited area of wife and mother.

URBAN WORKING-CLASS WOMEN

Compared with the Middle Ages, the independent professional activities of working-class women were more and more restricted during the Renaissance. From the late fifteenth century, stricter guild regulations gradually excluded women's participation in trades organized by guilds. This included most major commercial activities in towns. Because men in all trades objected to competition from lower-paid women, they tried to confine them to the least lucrative work. Furthermore, men were invading trades that had been traditionally exercised by women, for example, wholesale brewing. At this time occupational designations, with a few exceptions, such as the food and clothing trades, were male. By the sixteenth century, women were forbidden to become apprentices or to take the examinations that might have enabled them to become journeymen or masters. In the seventeenth and eighteenth centuries, new commercial organizations that were replacing the guilds were almost exclusively male dominated. Throughout most of Europe, women could not function on a professional basis independently of male relatives during the Renaissance era.

Given this discriminatory situation, it is not surprising to learn that the absolute numbers of women who were professional artists is very small in comparison with the number of male artists. In the sixteenth century, only 35 women are known to have been artists. The only women who became artists in Italy during the fifteenth century were nuns. In the sixteenth century, however, a few women of the upper class benefited from the dissemination of the educational principles of Castiglione, which insisted on training in the arts. Sofonisba Anguissola, for example, was born into an upper-class family that provided her with piano and drawing lessons, since these accomplishments were valued in women of her class. In addition to nuns in convents and noblewomen, daughters of artists also had access to artistic training. Artemisia Gentileschi and Angelica Kauffman were both daughters of artists and received their initial instruction from their fathers.

The obstacles placed before aspiring young female artists were many: cultural mores that discouraged emotional independence, severely restricted legal and economic rights, and, perhaps most importantly, limited access to artistic training. Despite these difficulties, the number of active women artists continued to increase. By the seventeenth century, over two hundred women artists are known, and from the eighteenth century, almost three hundred names of women artists have survived.

From this growing group of professional artists, the painters and sculptors to be discussed in chapters four, five, six, and seven emerged to build their reputations and to create works that altered the course of the history of art.

chapter 4

Painters in Italy: 1550–1650

No major women artists were active during the early Renaissance in Italy. The first Italian woman to build an international reputation as a professional painter was Sofonisba Anguissola, who did not begin her career until the 1550s. The other artist to be discussed here is Artemisia Gentileschi, who painted in a style adapted from Caravaggio, one of the initiators of the Baroque period, in the early 1600s.

The scarcity of women artists in the fifteenth century can be explained by the changing conditions under which artists were trained and the ways in which they practiced their profession in the Renaissance. During the Middle Ages, men and women artists had been either monks or nuns who received their training in the monastery or convent. Unlike the medieval era, the most important male artists of the Renaissance were no longer monks but craftsmen exposed to the new, sophisticated knowledge circulating in the secular art world. However, women artists in Italy in the fifteenth century continued to be mostly nuns, as was the case in the Middle Ages. The seclusion of the convent at a time when stylistic changes were rapidly taking place was an insuperable handicap for women's artistic achievement. It was simply not possible for women to become first-rate artists in the early period of the Italian Renaissance.

Most artists in the early Renaissance came from an artisan or working-class background and were members of guilds. Predictably, one can infer from the artists' guild regulations in Italy that women were hardly ever active. Furthermore, by the fifteenth century, the study of the human body, especially the male nude (from corpses and live models) was an essential component of the artist's training. It was absolutely impossible for women to acquire such training. Artists were also expected to travel to art centers to study contemporary production. Such freedom of movement was also totally beyond the capabilities of most women.

As in the early and high Renaissance periods, the innovators of Mannerism were all male. This is not surprising because these styles were formulated in multifigured religious compositions. In this most prestigious category of art, women remained seriously handicapped by their inability to study the nude or to acquire systematic and thorough artistic training as apprentices. Deprived of the necessary training, women painters almost never won commissions for large-scale public works of art.

Mannerism coexisted in northern Italy, Flanders, and other parts of Europe along with a counter-Manneristic style that was characterized by a fidelity to natural appearances. In the provincial centers of northern Italy, local aristocrats often commissioned portraits. Portraiture, being less dependent on the study of the nude, was a more accessible type of painting for women. Sofonisba Anguissola is known primarily for her portraits, which are painted in the more realistic, counter-Manneristic style of her native northern Italy.

By 1600 two artists, Annibale Caracci and Caravaggio, had developed personal styles that are seen as jointly initiating a new era in painting known as Baroque. Caravaggio adapted his native northern Italian naturalistic tradition for his religious compositions in Rome. Avoiding fresco in favor of oil on canvas, Caravaggio developed a radically new style that employed a dramatic chiaroscuro and realistic genre detail.

One of the first and foremost artists to paint in the style of Caravaggio was Orazio Gentileschi. His daughter Artemisia was trained by her father and her style fits within the Caravaggist mode, but it shows power and originality.

Annibale Carracci and his followers excelled in fresco painting, employing a style dependent on life drawing. Because women could not study the nude or learn the technique of fresco painting as apprentices, it is not surprising that no women are to be found among the disciples of Carracci, who included such masters as Guido Reni and Guercino. By 1625, the Bolognese followers of Annibale Carracci had captured all the major fresco commissions in Rome while the Caravaggists, such as Artemisia Gentileschi, were forced either to travel to other cities or content themselves with less lucrative private commissions.

SOFONISBA ANGUISSOLA
(ca. 1532–1625)

In the history of art, Sofonisba Anguissola is an important figure not only for her personal achievements but also because she provided a role model for other Italian women aspiring to be artists. It is hardly coincidental that several other artists, for example, Lavinia Fontana, Fede Galizia, and Barbara Longhi, all from different cities in northern Italy, followed the example of Anguissola and became practicing artists in the latter half of the sixteenth century.

Fortunately, about fifty signed paintings, mostly portraits, have survived. This represents a substantial number of works for a woman artist of this period and permits us to assess Anguissola's artistic achievements.

Anguissola was raised in an exceptional environment that allowed her to develop her creative talents. The oldest of six daughters, she was born into a noble family in the provincial northern Italian city of Cremona. Following the advice popularized by Baldesare Castiglione in *The Courtier*, her family made sure to provide their daughter with instruction in painting and music, as befitted a woman of her class. In addition to lessons in painting, Anguissola was taught to play the spinet, and in several self-portraits she shows herself playing this keyboard instrument. One can imagine that her father, Amilcare, faced with the financial burden of providing dowries for six daughters, was highly motivated to cultivate their talents. In fact, the three oldest sisters all received instruction in painting. Endowed with the fortunate circumstances of her class background and birth, Sofonisba Anguissola was in an unusually favorable position to develop her talents beyond the level of accomplished amateur to that of professional painter.

Because it was not acceptable for a single woman of her class to travel unchaperoned to Rome or any of the major Italian art centers, Sofonisba and her sister Elena, the second daughter, studied with a local painter in Cremona, Bernardino Campi. Elena gave up her career to become a nun. The third daughter, Lucia, also became an accomplished painter, although very few works can be securely attributed to her.

Amilcare Anguissola actively promoted Sofonisba's career as an artist. Recognizing the limitations of her local training, he corresponded with Michelangelo, who was living in Rome. In 1557, he asked the famous master to send Sofonisba several drawings to copy in oil paint and return for his criticism. Clearly, Amilcare was concerned that his daughter be exposed to the instruction of the finest living artist in Italy.[1] On one occasion, Sofonisba sent Michelangelo a drawing she had made of a smiling girl, and asked for the master's criticism and advice. Michelangelo admired the work but challenged her to depict the more difficult subject of a crying boy. In response to this challenge, Anguissola created a drawing which cleverly juxtaposes the two subjects. This work, *Boy Being Pinched by a Crawfish, and Girl* (Figure 8), demonstrates Anguissola's ability to represent a range of emotions. The features of the boy were based on those of her young brother (the seventh sibling in the family). This drawing was presented to the duke of Florence, Cosimo de Medici, and had widespread influence. It was seen by other artists, including Vasari, and copies were made of it. It has been suggested that Anguissola's drawing inspired Caravaggio's *Boy Bitten by a Lizard*.[2]

Despite this long-distance contact with the renowned Michelangelo, the main influence on Anguissola's painting style derives from the local environment of Cremona. Surrounded by Milan, Brescia, and Parma, Cremona's painters were exposed to several strands of "verist" or naturalist styles prevalent in these art centers. Artists from this region of northern Italy retained an almost Flemish taste for the precise description of nonidealized forms, in religious painting as well as in portraiture. The stylizations of Mannerism, so dominant in central Italy, never completely overwhelmed this local tradition. Thus, Sofonisba's talents for realistic description and anecdote seen in her drawing of the crying boy reflect the style of her native city.

Paintings from the first period of Anguissola's career, prior to 1559, are mostly portraits of her family. One of the most interesting of these works, *Three Sisters Playing Chess* (1555), is an inventive composition for a group portrait (Figure 9). While

FIGURE 8.   SOFONISBA ANGUISSOLA. *Boy Pinched by a Crayfish*. Drawing. Galleria Nazionale de Capodimonte, Naples.

the older sister on the left looks directly at the viewer, the younger player with hand raised appears to be speaking to her. The third sister and a servant are spectators to the interchange. This painting may be the first "conversation piece," a type of group portrait that would gain wide popularity in subsequent centuries.[3]

One can clearly observe the differences between Mannerist portraiture and the style of northern Italian realism practiced by Anguissola by comparing the *Three Sisters Playing Chess* with a contemporary portrait by the Mannerist painter Agnolo Bronzino, a male artist employed by the Medici court in Florence. Bronzino's *Eleanora of Toledo and Her Son, Giovanni de Medici* (Figure 10) presents a monumental personage looking out at the viewer with a cool, aloof gaze. No hints of expression or emotion are conveyed in the dispassionate faces of Eleanora and her son. By contrast, Anguissola's group portrait depicts a variety of facial expressions: the cheerful smile of the younger sister in the center, and the friendly direct look of the sister on the left. Bronzino paints Eleanora with an idealized stylization. Her elongated hands, similar to those in Paramagianino's *Madonna of the Long Neck,* are the most obvious clues to the manipulation of his sitter's appearance. In fact, Bronzino's painting may bear little resemblance to the actual features of Eleanora and her son, whereas, Anguissola is obviously portraying members of her family with a more accurate realism. Anguissola depicts individuals with specific facial features, unlike Bronzino's painting, which presents an idealized beauty relatively independent of natural appearances. While most of the surface of Bronzino's portrait is taken up with

FIGURE 9.   SOFONISBA ANGUISSOLA. *Three of the Artist's Sisters Playing Chess.*
1554. Oil on canvas. 27 3/16 x 35 7/8''. Narodowe w Poznaniu.

the lavish brocade dress of Eleanora, Anguissola minimizes costume details to permit
the personalities of her sitters and their lively interchange to occupy the viewer's attention.

During the 1550s Anguissola painted an unusually large number of self-portraits. These paintings were a form of self-advertisement that was rewarded when, in
1559, she was invited to join the court of King Philip II of Spain. The governor of
Milan had mentioned Anguissola to the duke of Alba, an emissary of the Spanish
court. Anguissola's position as one of Spain's court portraitists fits into a pattern of artistic links between Spain and Italy in the mid-sixteenth century. There was a tradition
of importing foreign artists to Spain as well as of sending native Spanish artists to Italy
for training. Titian had been appointed as official court portraitist to King Charles V in
1533. In 1567, Philip II hired six Italian artists to work as fresco decorators on the
huge palace-mausoleum-monastery complex, the Escorial. The most famous artist
working in Spain at this time, El Greco, was trained in Italy. From the 1560s through
the eighteenth century many Italian artists worked on a number of royal projects for
the Spanish monarchy.

Anguissola remained at the Spanish court through the 1560s. Although no
paintings from this period have survived, we can document that she painted several
portraits of Queen Isabella, one of which was sent to Pope Pius IV. In 1569 she mar-

FIGURE 10.   AGNOLO BRONZINO. *Eleanora of To-ledo and Her Son, Giovanni de Medici*. c. 1550. Oil on wood. 45 1/4 x 37 3/4''. Galleria degli Uffizi, Firenze.

ried a Sicilian nobleman, Fabrizio de Moncada, with a dowry that had been provided in the queen's will. King Philip of Spain gave her in marriage and presented her with numerous gifts. Through her talents as a painter, Anguissola achieved both fame and fortune, and her example was emulated by other aspiring women artists.

Anguissola's renown rests primarily on her pioneering position as the first professional Italian woman painter. Aside from her artistic talents, which were exceptional, she altered the conventions of portrait painting. She injected an innovative liveliness and range of emotion into her intimate portraits of members of her family. Anguissola's distinction resides mainly in her ability to communicate emotions convincingly through facial expression, rather than in the development of a personal style or method of paint application. Her art anticipates the more overt emotional content of much Baroque imagery.

ARTEMISIA GENTILESCHI
(1593–ca. 1652)

Artemisia Gentileschi developed a forceful personal style that placed her among the leading artists of her generation who worked in the style of Caravaggio. She traveled a great deal and helped spread the Caravaggesque mode through Italy. The dispersal of her own paintings further extended her influence.

As the child of the successful painter Orazio Gentileschi, Artemisia had the advantage of being raised in an environment where she could acquire the basic technical skills necessary for a professional artist. And because Orazio was one of the four most important artists to adapt Caravaggio's style in the first decade of the seventeenth century, it is not surprising that Artemisia would also develop a Caravaggesque style. One of her earliest paintings, *Judith with Her Maidservant* (Pitti Palace), was copied from her father's version of this theme as a learning exercise.

Orazio must have recognized his limitations as a teacher for his talented daughter because he arranged for her to study perspective with Agostino Tassi, a successful artist and collaborator who was receiving major commissions for fresco decorations of Roman palaces. Tassi seduced and raped Artemisia and then promised to marry her. When it became clear that Tassi, a disreputable character with a prior criminal record, had no intentions of marrying her, Orazio sued Tassi. The trial took place in 1612 and lasted several months. One can only wonder at Orazio's motivation in bringing Tassi to court and publicizing the mortification of his daughter. Artemisia was tortured on the witness stand with thumbscrews, a seventeenth-century lie detector. Tassi was imprisoned for eight months, but the case was ultimately dismissed, leaving Artemisia publicly humiliated. For this she has born a reputation for licentiousness through the centuries.

Shortly after the trial, Artemisia married a Florentine and went to live in Florence. There was little Caravaggist painting in that city, and Gentileschi's presence stimulated Florentine artists to investigate the new expressive possibilities of Caravaggism.

One of her most impressive paintings from the Florentine period of her career is the dramatically baroque composition *Judith Decapitating Holofernes* (Figure 11). Judith, the Old Testament heroine, stole into the enemy camp of the Israelites, murdered the tyrant Holofernes, and then escaped with his head. This story was a popular subject among the Caravaggists because it provided a biblical anecdote that could serve as a genre theme of violence or suspense.

Artemisia was especially fascinated with the Judith story and painted at least six different versions of it. It is easy to understand, as has been frequently suggested, why this theme appealed to her. Through the daring deed of Judith, Artemisia was avenging her own betrayal and all the wrongs she had suffered. Judith was an ideal subject for Artemisia—a heroine with whom she could identify as a woman, a heroic figure for the artist to depict.

When one compares Gentileschi's *Judith Decapitating Holofernes* with Caravaggio's version of the theme (Figure 12), one can see both the extent of Gentileschi's assimilation of Caravaggio's style and the differences that reveal her own vigorous sense of drama and originality. Like Caravaggio, Gentileschi positions large-scale figures in the foreground and uses highlighted forms that emerge from a dark background. The women in both works are not idealized and details are realistic. Both artists have selected the gory moment of decapitation.

However, Gentileschi designed a composition that is much more dynamic and

FIGURE 11.   ARTEMISIA GENTILESCHI. *Judith De-capitating Holofernes*. 1615–20. Oil on canvas. 46 3/4 x 37 1/4''. Pitti Palace, Florence.

energetic. In Caravaggio's painting, the figures are positioned across the picture surface. Gentileschi's composition places the figures in depth and is much more compact, therefore being more dramatic. Caravaggio's old maidservant is peripheral to the action while Gentileschi's maid actively participates in the murder, holding Holofernes down. In Gentileschi's painting, the arms of all three figures intersect in the center of the canvas, fixing the viewer's attention inescapably on the grisly act. The position of Caravaggio's rather pretty, elegant Judith seems frozen; she is not exerting physical force to cut off the tyrant's head. By contrast, one can acutely sense the intensity of the physical effort that Judith and her maid bring to this act. The powerful, monumental, and robust anatomy of Gentileschi's women make this decapitation seem much more convincing than Caravaggio's version.

One notable characteristic of Gentileschi's talent is her excellent knowledge of female anatomy. Perhaps being raised in the home of an avant-garde painter, she had the opportunity to study the female nude in private, using a servant or even her own

FIGURE 12.   CARAVAGGIO. *Judith and Holofernes*. c. 1598. 144 x 195 cm. Rome Casa Coppi.

body as a model. Her knowledge of male anatomy was understandably less sophisticated. The drapery covering Holofernes's torso masks this weakness.

In 1621 Gentileschi returned to Rome where she found the situation of the Caravaggists considerably different than when she had left the city almost a decade earlier. The Bolognese followers of Carracci were winning most major commissions, and Artemisia Gentileschi was now one of the few major Caravaggist painters living in Rome.

One of her finest paintings, perhaps her masterpiece, *Judith and Maidservant with the Head of Holofernes* (Figure 13), was painted in Rome during the 1620s. In this work Gentileschi eschews the overt violence of her earlier painting, replacing it with a hushed suspense and quiet tension. Rather than freezing the moment of the decapitation, she paints the aftermath of the act. The deed is done, but danger is still present. The women must now escape from the enemy camp bearing the head.

Both women look toward the left, frozen for a second, perhaps anticipating imminent discovery. The position of Judith is particularly complex. While her right hand crosses her body, shielding the candlelight, her left hand holds the sword in tense readiness. The sword is placed in the exact center of the canvas. Composition and gestures, rather than facial expressions, convey the meaning. The work is painted with great sophistication. The complementary colors of the gown, yellow and purple, contrast beautifully with the ruby-red of the hanging drapery. The Caravaggesque chiaroscuro conveys an element of secrecy and mystery to the scene. The light reveals

FIGURE 13. ARTEMISIA GENTILESCHI. Italian, 1593–c. 1651. *Judith and Maidservant with the Head of Holofernes.* c. 1625. Oil on canvas. H.: 6'1/2'' W.: 55 3/4''. 52.253. H.: 1.842m W.: 1.416m. Gift of Mr. Leslie H. Green. Courtesy of The Detroit Institute of Arts.

the forms of the women, but the rest of the canvas is cast in darkness so that the viewer must inevitably focus on Judith and her maid.

The story of Judith was not the only subject in which Gentileschi invented new compositions or discovered new layers of meaning based on her identity as a woman. In an extremely unusual painting, Gentileschi painted herself as the living embodiment of "Painting." In *Self-Portrait as the Allegory of Painting* (Figure 14), Gentileschi depicts herself bearing the widely recognized attributes that identify the allegorical figure "Painting" in this era: on the gold chain hangs a mask standing for imitation; her unkempt hair symbolizes the divine frenzy of the creator; and her multicolored dress demonstrates the painter's talents. The artist is not actually painting but is poised facing the light flooding her from an unknown source. She is waiting for inspiration or summoning her mental energies:

FIGURE 14.   ARTEMISIA GENTILESCHI. *Self-Portrait as the Allegory of Painting.* Oil on canvas. 38 1/2 x 29 1/2''. St. James's Palace, London. Copyright reserved.

> Without recourse to complex personification, Artemisia evokes the contrast between Theory and Practice in her *Self-Portrait*. She has posed herself with one arm raised upward, the hand stretched toward its invisible target, suggesting the higher, ideal aspirations of painting, with the other arm resting firmly on a table, the hand holding the brushes and palette which are the physical materials of painting.[4]

Unlike male artists, who were forced to depict themselves accompanied by a symbolic female figure symbolizing Painting, Artemisia, as a woman artist, could combine her image with the iconography of the allegorical personification of painting and create a deceptively simple composition of great iconographic originality.

Unwilling to abandon her personal style of Caravaggism to accommodate the changing tastes of Roman patrons, Gentileschi traveled to Naples in 1630. Except for a brief visit to London to assist her ailing father on a commission, she lived in Naples for the rest of her life. The selection of Naples as her next residence was logical because more artists worked in a Caravaggist style there for a longer period of time than in any other Italian city. In fact, between 1600 and 1630, Caravaggism was the only advanced painting style practiced in Naples. However, this situation was to change during the 1630s when the influence of the Bolognese school, especially the art of Guido Reni, became increasingly important, even in Naples. Accepting the inevitable, Gentileschi now adapted her style to the more brightly illuminated, idealized mode of the Caracci followers. In the process she lost some of the intensity of her personal style. Scholars generally agree that the works created in her original Caravaggist mode are her finest paintings.

The sheer formal beauty and power of many of Artemisia Gentileschi's paintings serves to rank her with the best artists of her generation. Never a mere imitator of Caravaggio, she adapted some of that artist's devices to forge an original style of strength and beauty. Her inventive adaptations of existing subjects is another aspect of her originality. She harnessed her formal energies to the expression of a personal iconography, expressing her identity as a woman and as an artist.

chapter 5

Seventeenth-Century Dutch and Flemish Artists

The careers of the four artists discussed in this chapter demonstrate the level of excellence that may be achieved by women artists when the expectations for women in their culture do not conflict with a measure of equality of opportunity and access to training. Clara Peeters, an important figure in the first generation of independent still life artists, was born in Antwerp, but her later works reflect contemporary developments in Holland. Judith Leyster, a contemporary of Frans Hals, one of the major portrait painters of the century, lived and worked in Haarlem. Leyster is an atypical Dutch artist because she painted a variety of types of works, including still lifes, genre scenes, and portraits, all with equal quality and inventiveness. Maria Sibylla Merian is generally considered the finest botanical illustrator of her time. Although she was born in Frankfurt, Germany, both her stepfather and her husband were Flemish flower painters. After 1690 she lived in Amsterdam, and her connections with the traditions of Dutch and Flemish illustration are sufficiently strong to warrant her placement in this context. Independent flower paintings gained wide popularity in both Flanders and Holland. By the early eighteenth century, the Dutch painter Rachel Ruysch was one of the most famous flower painters of her era.

Holland secured her independence from Spain in 1581 and by the seventeenth century was the major maritime power of Europe, with a far-flung colonial empire. Because Holland was a Protestant country, the Church was not an active arts patron as it remained to some extent in neighboring Catholic Flanders. However, the Dutch middle class was wealthy and purchased paintings on a regular basis. This provided a strong incentive for Dutch artists to paint the kinds of works that would appeal to the merchants of the middle class—their only source of patronage.

Because these works of art were intended to adorn the burghers' homes, the vast majority of Dutch paintings are small-scaled, suitable for hanging in private houses. With the exception of portraits, paintings were sold on the open market, creating a competitive situation that kept prices low. In this context, painters developed precise areas of specialization, such as still life painting, flower arrangements, landscapes, seascapes, and genre paintings, in an effort to secure a steady market. The unifying factor in all these categories was a dependence on precisely observed natural phenomena. Dutch art is characterized stylistically by its realism. The Dutch created a body of works that humanized art. ''Works by a large number of painters reflected the common experiences of life in all their diversity. In concrete terms, they embraced the typical, the ordinary, in human concerns.''[1] Rembrandt is, of course, the most famous and most individual genius in seventeenth-century Dutch painting. He is not an isolated genius because he lived in a period of great productivity stimulated by the open market economy. At that time, painting schools were flourishing in Utrecht, Haarlem, Amsterdam, Leiden, Delft, and other cities in Holland.

This competitive art market created an advantageous situation for women artists. Artists could paint what they liked and when they liked, rather than painting only when commissioned. Any artist could accept as many pupils as he wished. Although the guilds were the primary artists' organizations, there were considerably fewer restrictions on who could become an artist in Holland than in other parts of Europe. Furthermore, with the development of the new painting specialities mentioned earlier, there was no need to study the nude; in fact, there are very few nudes in Dutch art.

Still life and flower painting did not require knowledge of anatomy or extensive travel to Italy to study the High Renaissance masters. Throughout Europe, women were in the forefront of still life painting in the early 1600s. Only a still life attributed to Caravaggio is known to predate the works of Fede Galizia in Italy. In France, Louise Moillon painted a series of impressive still lifes, and four women painters of still lifes were elected to the French Academy during the seventeenth century. However, the most noteworthy women still life painters were Flemish and Dutch, since these schools were the most active and suffered least from the French Academy's low esteem for this genre.

The origins of still life painting date back to early fifteenth-century Netherlandish religious paintings. In the *Merode Altarpiece,* the Master of Flemalle included a number of objects—a silver candlestick, a porcelain vase with lilies, a polished brass pot and towel—all painted with great precision. While each object has a symbolic significance related to Mary, the prominence of these inanimate things in a religious work demonstrates a Netherlandish fascination with the illusionistic description of everyday objects. This tradition continues in the work of Hugo van der Goes, who positions two vases of flowers and a sheaf of wheat prominently in the foreground of his masterpiece, the *Portinari Altarpiece.* Here again, each item has a symbolic meaning: the scarlet lily symbolizes the blood of the Passion; the columbine, a symbol of sorrow, refers to a prophecy of Mary's future grief; and the wheat is both a literal translation of ''Bethlehem, which means ''House of Bread'' in Hebrew, and a symbol of the Eucharist.

The earliest independent still life and flower paintings date from the mid-sixteenth century. Jan Brueghel, in Antwerp, is credited with the invention of independent flower paintings. He created a series of works that depict a single vase of flowers symmetrically arranged, isolated, and set against a dark background.

Flower painters regularly juxtaposed blossoms that could never bloom simultaneously in nature. Each flower was studied individually. Assembling these studies in the studio, the painter created imaginary bouquets. By 1600 the cultivation of flowers as a commodity had become an important component of the Dutch economy. A highly speculative market developed and huge sums were paid for rare tulip bulbs. Prices became so inflated that the market crashed in the 1630s. (The term "tulipomania" is still used today to designate a highly speculative commodity market.)

Painters incorporated into their works the new floral species that were brought back to Europe from the voyages of discovery around the globe. The East and West India Companies were expanding the Dutch colonial empire at this time. The introduction and cultivation of exotic species, not native to Europe, further stimulated contemporary interest in flower painting. As the prosperity of the merchant class increased, there was widespread interest in gardening and the cultivation of flowers, including new and familiar types. All these factors combined to create an especially strong interest in the Netherlands for paintings of flowers.

Another way to account for the widespread interest in flowers is that these fragile objects, which bloom and die so quickly, are universal symbols of life's transience. Whether combined with other objects, associated with the vanity of earthly existence, or standing alone, flowers express in a gentle, beautiful manner the connotations of imminent mortality.

One of the most important artists to continue the tradition of the independent flower painting was Jacques de Gheyn. Born in Antwerp, he lived and worked in various cities in Holland. In 1606 the Dutch government commissioned a flower piece from him for the large sum of 600 guilders, to be presented to Marie de Medici, queen of France. This placed de Gheyn among the best paid artists of his time and indicates the high level of esteem for this type of painting. It is easy to see, then, that when Clara Peeters included bouquets of flowers in her still life pictures, she was both demonstrating her versatility and increasing the marketability of her canvases.

CLARA PEETERS (1594–ca. 1657)

Clara Peeters was one of the originators of a type of still life painting known as the "breakfast" or "banquet" piece. She often included vases of flowers in these compositions, demonstrating the versatility of her talent. The origins of the "banquet" still life can be traced back to the paintings of Pieter Aertsen and his nephew, Joachim Beuckelaer, in Amsterdam. In the mid-sixteenth century, these artists created paintings displaying lavish quantities of meats, fish, fruits, and other edibles, and generally including a small religious scene in the background.

During the course of the sixteenth century, these small scenes disappear entirely, and a table filled with food stands alone. Only a handful of such independent "banquet" or "breakfast" pieces can be securely dated before 1608. This is the year of the earliest known banquet piece by Clara Peeters. From this evidence, she can be identified as one of the inventors of this type of still life. By 1611 Peeters was painting works that demonstrate a superb talent for rendering details of texture and form in a wide range of objects.

We don't know very much about the life of Clara Peeters. She was born in 1594 in Antwerp, the art capital of the Netherlands, and displayed a talent for painting at a very early age. Her first works were painted when she was only fourteen. In all likelihood her family decided to encourage her artistic talents rather than marry her off at the usual age of twenty. Actually, Peeters did not marry until she was forty-five, and then probably because it had become too difficult for her to continue to support herself solely from painting. In fact, in this highly competitive art market even the most talented and successful artists had to supplement their incomes regularly from other sources. Aside from her date of birth and date of marriage, there is scant information available about Peeters' career. Had she been a man, there would undoubtedly be more documentation preserved in the Antwerp guild records.

As to her training, we do not know how Peeters acquired her skills. It is possible that she studied with Osias Beert, fourteen years her senior, who was a noted still life painter in Antwerp. Her works relate to those of Beert in the combination of different types of objects: flowers, fruits, tall decorative metal goblets, and flat dishes of fruits. Peeters, however, uses a lower viewpoint than Beert or other Flemish colleagues. With this lowered viewpoint, she employs more accurate perspective to situate the objects firmly in space. The illusion of the arrangement is thus enhanced. This composition also differs from those of her immediate contemporaries in that she groups her objects closer together, permitting a certain amount of overlapping. These elements anticipated the subsequent development of the banquet pieces of artists such as Pieter Claesz and Willem Claesz Heda.

Peeters' innovations are evident in *Still Life with Flowers, A Goblet, Dried Fruit and Pretzels* (Figure 15). This painting is part of a series of four complex works, each focused around a different theme: a fish piece, a game piece, a dinner arrangement, and the work illustrated here. These paintings are recognized as among the masterpieces of early seventeenth-century still life, yet they were painted by an artist only seventeen years old. The work reproduced here is typical of every known painting by Peeters in its use of a simple stone ledge set against a dark background. An elaborate goblet defines the center of the composition. The central focus is underscored by the low dish filled with dried fruits and nuts. The vase of flowers on the left is counterbalanced by a plate of pretzels, a pewter pitcher, and a glass. The placement of these objects results in a balanced composition that is not symmetrical or monotonous. Each object is rendered in a precise style that conveys clearly the diverse textures of the objects.

In a still life painted the following year, 1612, Peeters uses similar objects but arranges them in a more restrained composition. Instead of the complex, *horror vacui* of the Prado painting (Figure 15), the *Still Life with a Vase of Flowers, Goblets, and Shells* (Figure 16) is rather austere. This painting, often considered Peeters' masterpiece, depicts three tall objects—on the right, the same goblet as in the Prado painting, another goblet in the center, and a vase of flowers on the left. A single tulip, gold coins, a low dish, and some seashells rest on the ledge anchoring the vertical forms. By positioning the vase of flowers to one side rather than framing it with the goblets,

FIGURE 15. CLARA PEETERS. *Still Life with Flowers, a Goblet, Dried Fruit and Pretzels*. 1611. Oil on panel. 19 11/16 x 28 5/16''. Prado Museum, Madrid.

FIGURE 16. CLARA PEETERS. *Still Life with a Vase of Flowers, Goblets, and Shells*. 1612. Oil on panel. 23 7/16 x 19 5/16''. Karlsruhe, Staatliche Kunsthalle.

Peeters established a dynamic composition. The height of the flowers competes with the height of the metal forms. All three vertical objects are placed at different points in depth, further energizing the composition. The work is technically brilliant. The artist has even included her own image reflected seven times in the surface of the goblet on the right. (The use of the self-portrait as a form of advertisement was noted in connection with Sofonisba Anguissola.) Shells, often transported from exotic places, were collector's items of the era. In this work the wonders of nature, i.e., flowers and shells, are juxtaposed against beautifully wrought metal chalices, testimony to the creative skills of man.

After 1620, Peeters painted much simpler arrangements of cheeses and humble objects. Her color scheme becomes monochromatic, reflecting contemporary Dutch tastes.

The surviving signed and dated works by Peeters are sufficiently numerous to permit the assessment of her talent. Born in the active art center of Antwerp during its golden age, she created a series of paintings that reveal great technical proficiency and originality in composition.

JUDITH LEYSTER (1609–1660)

Unlike most of her colleagues, Judith Leyster did not specialize in one specific type of painting. She was a versatile artist who painted still lifes, portraits, and genre paintings. The body of works that can be securely attributed to her demonstrates that Leyster was a talented painter who could invent interesting compositions as well as re-interpret conventional subjects from a woman's perspective.

Leyster's father owned a brewery in Haarlem. Despite the fact that she was not born into an artistic family, she managed to receive an adequate training, although it is not known with whom she studied. In 1628 Leyster's family moved to a town near Utrecht. Utrecht had an active school of painters who were familiar with Caravaggio's innovations. Utrecht artists, such as Terbruggen or Honthorst, often used artificial light to illuminate their religious or genre scenes. In many of Leyster's subsequent paintings she adapts this indirect light source.

In 1629 Leyster and her family returned to Haarlem, where she lived until 1636. She became a member of the Haarlem painters' guild in 1633, and most of her surviving paintings date from this period of her life. In 1636 she married a fellow painter, Jan Meinse Molenaer (1610–1668), and the couple moved to Amsterdam where she bore three children. It is not certain why her artistic production declined so dramatically after her marriage. Despite the decline in her production, an adequate number of paintings survive to permit an evaluation of Leyster's position in the active art world of seventeenth-century Holland.

Leyster's *Self-Portrait* (Figure 17) is a characteristic example of her style. In this work, she proclaims her identity as a painter. Holding a palette and brushes, she sits in front of a picture of a laughing musician, one of her specialties in genre painting.

FIGURE 17. JUDITH LEYSTER. *Self-Portrait.* c. 1635. Oil on canvas. 29 3/8 x 25 5/8''. National Gallery of Art, Washington. Gift of Mr. and Mrs. Robert Woods Bliss.

The style of Judith Leyster has been frequently compared to that of her more famous Haarlem contemporary, Frans Hals—usually to Leyster's disadvantage. In 1631 she served as a witness for the baptism of one of Hals' children, so we can assume that she knew Hals' work. When one compares Leyster's *Self-Portrait* with *Malle Babbe* by Hals (Figure 18), both the similarities and differences between the works of these two artists may be observed. In both paintings, the figures are positioned in a three-quarter view, set very close to the foreground, while the bottom edge of the picture cuts the figure just below the waist. They sit before undetailed monochromatic backgrounds that do not distract the viewer's attention from the main figures. Both works convey a fresh immediacy, almost as if the sitter had been captured in a snapshot photograph. Such similarities are predictable in works by two artists living in the same time and place.

The differences between these two paintings underscore the extent of Leyster's originality. Hals' *Malle Babbe* reveals a free and active brushwork over most of the

FIGURE 18. FRANS HALS. *Malle Babbe.* c. 1650. Oil on canvas. 29½ x 25″. State Museums, Berlin-Dahlem. Photo: Jörg P. Anders.

surface. In fact, this painterly technique is the single quality that has earned Hals his reputation in the history of art. A recent scholar admits that Hals was ''limited in his interests and subject matter, limited in his formal invention, but brilliant in his brushwork.''[2] Hals' active brushwork unifies the painting surface of *Malle Babbe* but results inevitably in the suppression of the sense of different textures of the pewter tankard, black cloth, dress, and lace ruff. The style of Leyster's *Self-Portrait* is more precise and linear. While she does use visible brushstrokes in her lace cuffs and skirt, she generally does not allow the texture of the paint to intrude upon the description of the variety of textures included in her image. Twentieth-century tastes, trained by exposure to Impressionism and subsequent avant-garde art movements, tend to value Hals' spontaneous, sketch-like style. However, Leyster's technique would have been at least equally valued in her own time. In fact, the popularity and skill of an artist was measured in large part by the technical ability to depict a wide range of objects and textures. Therefore, it is not warranted to condemn Leyster's style as inferior when it reveals traits that would have been valued by her own culture. Clearly, despite superficial similarities, Leyster's technique is quite distinct from Hals'. She is not a mere imitator, but an independent artist with a personal style.

While Hals painted only portraits, Leyster painted genre scenes as well. In one of her most famous genre pictures, *The Proposition* (Figure 19), she invents a new content for a familiar subject.[3] The painting depicts a man in a fur hat, leaning over a woman who is sewing. He is offering her gold coins as payment for her sexual favors. The bare interior focuses the viewer's attention on this scene, which is illuminated by a single candle.

The use of a sharply focused artificial light source relates to the influence of the Utrecht Caravaggists on Leyster's style. However, the light source is the only similarity between *The Proposition* and the scenes of prostitution and procurement that are common among the artists of the Utrecht school. When one compares *The Proposi-*

FIGURE 19. JUDITH LEYSTER. *The Proposition.* 1631. Oil on panel. 11 11/16 x 9 1/2''. Mauritshuis, The Hague.

tion with Dirck van Baburen's *The Procuress* (Figure 20), a wholly different content is immediately apparent. The woman in Baburen's image is a willing prostitute exchanging her favors for the gold coin offered by the male customer. Her low-cut dress reveals her physical attributes. The musical instrument, especially the lute, is a familiar prop in themes of prostitution since music is always associated with Venus and love-making. The old procuress on the right holds out her hand, waiting for payment for the prostitute's services. The mood is clearly jovial and animated.

By contrast, the woman in *The Proposition* is the embarassed victim of an undesired solicitation. There are no wine glasses or musical instruments, common attributes of brothel scenes. Instead, the modestly dressed woman fixedly concentrates on her sewing. Her feet rest on a footwarmer, further emphasizing the immobility of her pose. In this work, Leyster invented a new interpretation of a genre subject that is more empathetic to women than the paintings of her male colleagues. She conceives of an interaction in which an ordinary woman chooses honor over money. Leyster, as

FIGURE 20. DIRCK VAN BABUREN. *The Procuress*. Dutch fl. 1611—d. 1623. Oil on canvas. 39 3/4 x 42 1/4'' (101 x 107.5 cm.). 50.2721, Purchased, Maria T. B. Hopkins Fund. Courtesy, Museum of Fine Arts, Boston.

a woman, could realize more clearly than her male contemporaries that not every proposition occurs between willing participants.

The restrained, quiet mood of *The Proposition* may have influenced the next generation of genre painters, including Vermeer and Metsu. In several works, Metsu explores the theme of a sensitive woman victimized by a coarser man, while Vermeer became a master in the intimate domestic scene in which men interrupt women at their work. Both themes are anticipated in Leyster's painting.

Judith Leyster's works demonstrate her ability to combine influences from the Utrecht Caravaggists with her local Haarlem traditions, epitomized by the art of Hals into a personal style of variety, beauty, and iconographic originality.

MARIA SIBYLLA MERIAN (1647–1717)

The history of the science of botany is closely related to the development of flower painting. The documentation and categorization of the many new species of flowers was necessarily dependent on the accurate illustration of each specimen. The original drawings, in watercolor, were reproduced through woodcuts or engravings, and sometimes bound into books.

By the late fifteenth and early sixteenth century, two important artists, Leonardo da Vinci and Albrecht Dürer had recorded the characteristics of different plants with scientific precision. In the mid-sixteenth century, the Flemish artist Georg Hoefnagle (1542–1600) painted book illuminations in watercolor, describing rare species of flowers and insects with a naturalist's accuracy of detail. By the seventeenth century, many artists worked on a number of volumes that documented the hundreds of new flowers imported from other countries in Europe as well as the New World. In fact, travel to foreign lands was an integral component of the interest in flower paintings as well as the rationale for their documentation in botanical drawings.

The close historical connection between the science of botany and the illustration of flowers is especially relevant for an understanding of the achievements of Maria Sibylla Merian. One of the finest botanical artists of the period, she eventually extended her interests to include the scientific study and illustration of insects and animals as well. Her contributions to the history of entomology and botany have long been recognized. More recently, her position in the history of art is also being reevaluated because her scientific contribution was conveyed through impressive visual images.

Matthaus Merian, Maria's father, was an engraver who published one of the first collections of flower illustrations in 1641. Although Matthaus died in 1650, when Maria was only three, his work provided the inspiration for her first major publication, the three volume *New Flower Book,* completed in 1680. Maria's mother soon remarried Jacob Marell, a fine Flemish flower painter. One of Marell's students, Johann Andreas Graff, married Maria in 1665. With the advantages of this background, Maria Merian easily received a sophisticated training in the art of flower painting.

Her first completely original publication was *The Wonderful Transformation of Caterpillars and Their Singular Plant Nourishment,* published in 1679. (Two additional volumes were later published.) In this work, the development from larvae to caterpillar to moth of 186 varieties of European insects is illustrated. Each species is depicted with its preferred plant. Maria collected the insect eggs and studied the life cycle of each moth. This was the first time that scientific precision was brought to the investigation of the insect world. Prior to the publication of these volumes, there was no understanding of the life cycles of insects. "Merian thus revolutionized the sciences of zoology and botany and laid the foundations for the classification of plant and animal species made by Charles Linnaeus in the eighteenth century."[4]

Merian lived in Nuremberg from 1670 to 1685. She then resided with a religious sect, the Labadists, for several years, eventually settling in Amsterdam in 1690. There she studied the available insect collections, including that of Professor Frederik Ruysch, Rachel's father. While Rachel Ruysch was very precise in her depictions of plants, animals, and insects, her images, as we shall see, are artificial constructions, without the spirit of scientific inquiry that Merian brought to her study of nature.

In 1699 Merian left Amsterdam accompanied by her daughter and traveled to the Dutch colony of Surinam in South America on a scientific research mission sponsored by the city of Amsterdam. One can imagine the courage and professional dedication that motivated Merian, unaccompanied by any male protector, to undertake such a long and dangerous voyage to a far off tropical colony. Over the next two years, Merian collected a wide range of specimens of the insects, plants, and animals of Surinam. With anthropological interest, she recorded the customs of the natives as well. After becoming seriously ill, she returned to Amsterdam with her daughter. Four years later, in 1705, the first volume of her masterpiece, *Metamorphosis insectorum Surinamsium,* was published. The author of a history of botanical illustration calls it "magnificent."[5] The work consists of 60 large plates, engraved from Merian's watercolors. Some copies were hand colored by Merian herself. Each plate is accompanied by a detailed description, written by the artist/author.

Plate V (Figure 21) is a characteristic example of the images in this work. The composition is designed to include the maximum amount of information without sacrificing clarity and legibility. Plate V presents a caterpillar striped black and yellow, with red head and tail. Merian's commentary informs us that this caterpillar shed its skin in December 1700 and was transformed into the brown and white moth positioned at the upper right. The moth is rendered with precision and delicacy. This species of caterpillar feeds on the Cassaba plant (breadfruit), which dominates the composition. Merian shows the root system, stem and leaves, and provides a description of the preparation of breadfruit, a dietary staple of the native population, prepared from the roots of this plant. The artist's more purely aesthetic instincts are shown by the depiction of a writhing, coiled snake. The snake eggs are located in the lower left. These eggs do not have a shell, but rather a skin, like crocodile and tortoise eggs.

FIGURE 21. MARIA SIBYL-
LA MERIAN. *Metamorphosis
Insectorum Surinamsium*, Plate
V. 1705. Hand-colored engrav-
ing. Library, The Academy of
Natural Sciences of Philadelphia.

Within a unified and beautiful composition, Merian has compressed an extraordinary wealth of scientific information. While her main purpose was the expansion of
scientific knowledge, she raised the level of botanical illustration to that of fine art.
Coming from a family of flower painters, Merian possessed a highly refined formal
sensibility. Her remarkable achievement in the history of botany and entomology also
deserves recognition in the history of art.

RACHEL RUYSCH (1666–1750)

While other types of still life painting became less popular in Holland, by the late
seventeenth-century flower pictures retained their desirability and popularity. The
Dutch continued to cultivate a wide variety of species of flowers for business and
pleasure during the 1600s. The prosperity of the merchant class encouraged the prolif-
eration of private gardens where new varieties of flowers were eagerly sought and cultivated. Patrons often wanted flower painters to record their best or rarest blossoms.

Rachel Ruysch and Jan van Huysum were the two most prominent and successful painters specializing in flower pictures in the late seventeenth and early eighteenth
centuries. Ruysch's complex paintings of flowers, fruits, and fauna were widely ad-

FIGURE 23.   RACHEL RUY-
SCH. *Fruit, Flowers, and In-
sects.* 1716. Oil on canvas.
Palazzo Pitti, Firenze.

great Flemish and Dutch flower painters. Towering over her contemporaries, she enjoyed a highly productive and successful career. Her works are never monotonous.
She maintained a consistently high level of excellence in paintings that reveal a range
of dynamic compositional formulas. Using a wide variety of plants, insects, fruits,
etc., she created monumental paintings of widely recognized and enduring quality.

chapter 6

Eighteenth-Century Italian and French Painters

The three artists discussed in this chapter were specialists in portraiture and still life. As noted in the preceding chapter, these painting genres were based on direct observation and were therefore more accessible to women artists. Rosalba Carriera, a Venetian, did not suffer severely from a lack of proper training. She worked in two media, pastel portraiture and miniature painting on ivory, in which she invented the techniques particular to her art. Anne Vallayer-Coster, a still life and flower painter, and Elisabeth Vigée-Lebrun, a portraitist, were daughters of artists who were raised in Paris and learned to paint at home.

From 1661 until the beginning of the eighteenth century, France was ruled by one of its most powerful monarchs, Louis XIV. Aided by his minister, Colbert, Louis established a highly centralized bureaucracy. Unlike the bourgeois republic of Holland, France was an absolute monarchy. These different political systems profoundly affected the lives of professional artists, the types of art produced, and the opportunities for women artists to receive training.

As opposed to the situation in Holland, where the Dutch middle classes were avid consumers of paintings, virtually all commissions in France came from the monarchy. There was little diversity or scope for personal styles. Louis XIV believed that the arts, like the sciences, industries, and other activities, should serve the glory of France and her king. Through a reorganization of the Paris Academy in 1663, the fine arts were brought under the direct control of the state bureaucracy. Early in Louis' reign, he decided to create a magnificent setting for himself and his court at Versailles. Most of the efforts of French artists of this era were directed toward the embellishment of this enormous palace. Only male painters were permitted to receive the training necessary to create the large-scale history paintings that decorated the walls and ceilings at Versailles. Control over artists was easily maintained because all artists working for the king had to be members of the Academy.

Given the inflexibility of this system of education and patronage, it is not surprising to find no women artists of major significance in France during the seventeenth century. Denied access to the training essential for a professional artist, the highly structured, state controlled art world of Louis XIV effectively prevented any women from achieving excellence. Because there was no real market for other types of paintings, few artists specialized in those genres popular in Holland, such as flower painting, still life, and small-scale portraiture, types of art in which women often excelled.

The decentralization and loosening of state control over the arts that occurred in France following the death of Louis XIV in the period known as the "Rococo" created a much more favorable environment for women artists.

The aristocratic clientele, which eagerly purchased the intimate and sensuous paintings of the Rococo masters to decorate their newly built Parisian townhouses, also supported the art of portraiture. By the 1720s, Carriera had built an international reputation for her pastel portraits. In 1720 she became the only foreign woman to be elected to the French Academy. Similarly, in the decade prior to the French Revolution, Vigée-Lebrun was the most successful portrait artist of the aristocracy. In the 1780s she became Queen Marie Antoinette's official court painter.

During the eighteenth century, a new appreciation for still life and flower paintings developed among the same French aristocrats who supported portraiture. Chardin, the most famous still life painter in France in the 1700s, had a long, honorable, and successful career. Despite the fact that he painted only still lifes and genre scenes, he was accepted into the French Academy in 1728. Vallayer-Coster, a contemporary of Chardin's, also had an active and respected career as a still life painter. She was accepted into the Academy in 1770 at the early age of 26.

ROSALBA CARRIERA (1675–1752)

Rosalba Carriera's special contribution to the history of art was her invention of a new type of art form, the pastel portrait. Her influence in this medium was very widespread, and she won international renown. Carriera's life-size portraits in colored chalks did not merely reflect the Rococo qualities of her epoch, but they contributed to the formation of the tastes of her society. Carriera made an equally important innovation in miniature painting. She was the first artist to use ivory as a support for miniature portraits. Ivory had marked advantages over parchment, both for durability and luminosity, and it was therefore widely adopted by miniature painters during the eighteenth century.

Carriera rose from very humble origins to become one of the most successful artists of her epoch. She was born in Venice; her father was a clerk and her mother, a lacemaker. Harris and Nochlin suggest that she began her career by learning the art of lace making and when this industry declined, shifted to the decoration of ivory snuffboxes.[1] These inexpensive items were produced in mass quantities for the tourist trade. From this initiation, Carriera became familiar with painting on ivory in a small scale, and she began to create miniature portraits.

As a miniature painter, Carriera possessed great skill in rendering detail and in applying the paint in a range of thicknesses. Her active brushwork revolutionized the style of miniature painting and certainly contributed to her success. *Venus and Cupid* (Figure 24) is a characteristic example of her miniature style. The modeling of the figures is rendered in a combined technique of painted shadows and tiny dots. The drapery partially covering Venus is painted in a thicker, more active impasto.

Miniature painting has suffered from low esteem in the history of art, despite the fact that miniaturization requires an especially precise technical control. Because they are small, miniatures are often seen as inherently less "significant" than larger scale paintings. Clearly, painting in miniature is a difficult task to perform because the small size of the image forces the artist to exercise extraordinary manual control. The eyestrain that this work inevitably involved may well have contributed to Carriera's loss of sight in 1746. She spent the last years of her life blind and in seclusion, suffering from periods of depression.

Carriera's first professional successes were in the medium of miniature painting, but she achieved international renown for her pastel portraits. Although colored chalks, known as pastels, had been invented in the late fifteenth century, no artist before Carriera had explored their formal possibilities. Employing pastels in an unprecedented way, she skillfully created a naturalistic range of textures. At the invitation

FIGURE 24. ROSALBA CAR-RIERA. *Venus and Cupid*. Miniature on ivory. 4 1/16 x 3 3/8''. Statens Museum For Kunst, Copenhagen.

of a Parisian banker, whom she had met in Venice, she arrived in Paris in 1720. One of her first portraits was of the young French king, Louis XV (Figure 25). The portrait was greeted with widespread admiration. This image reveals a detailed, highly finished, and almost oil-paint-like treatment of the face combined with a more spontaneous technique in the jacket, cravat, and hair. In these sections, one can actually see the individual marks of the chalk. This precision, combined with a freedom of touch not achievable in oils, amazed her audience in Paris. In recognition of her achievements, she was invited to become a member of the French Academy—a great honor for any artist, and an unprecedented one for a foreign woman. Despite her warm reception in France, Carriera decided to return to her native Venice in 1721.

As a portrait artist, Carriera's talents were widely appreciated by an international clientele. Europe's aristocracy demanded portraits by her hand. The king of Denmark and many members of England's upper classes were among her patrons, while Augustus III, Elector of Saxony and King of Poland, collected more than 150 of her works.

FIGURE 25. ROSALBA CARRIERA. Italian. *Louis XV as a Boy*. Pastel on paper. 19 x 14". 65.2655, Forsyth Wickes Collection. Courtesy, Museum of Fine Arts, Boston.

Carriera possessed a refined color sense. She often used bright, fresh colors for a brilliant, luminous effect. This specific aspect of her style relates her art to that of her Venetian contemporary, Tiepolo. Tiepolo also worked for foreign patrons, but unlike Carriera, Tiepolo regularly executed large-scale mural decorations.

A special flair of Carriera's was her ability to make a flattering image of her sitter without losing his or her individual likeness. This ability was essential for an eighteenth-century portraitist, when a portrait often served the purpose that a photograph does today. The duke of Modena, aware of Carriera's success in Paris, commissioned the artist to paint portraits of his three marriageable daughters. These portraits were circulated to attract eligible suitors who could form advantageous political alliances with the duke.[2] Clearly, a flattering image was not merely a matter of vanity but, as in this case, a political strategy as well.

When Carriera did not have the restrictions of a commissioned portrait, she was capable of a forthright realism. This quality is most clearly apparent in her self-portraits. The strong image of herself shown here (Figure 26) was made shortly before

FIGURE 26. ROSALBA CARRIERA. *Self-Portrait*. Pastel on paper. Gallerie Dell'Accademia, Venezia.

she went blind. This work reveals honesty, sharp powers of observation, and un-flinching precision.

Carriera's name resounded through the eighteenth century and she paved the way, as a role model if not as a direct influence, for other portrait painters. Masters of pastel portraiture, such as Maurice Quentin de la Tour and Jean-Baptiste Perroneau, are among the inheritors of her invention. Contemporaries of Vigée-Lebrun and Labille-Guiard regularly compared these artists, active later in the eighteenth century, with Carriera. Theresa Concordia Mengs, Suzanne Giroust-Roslin, Labille-Guiard and her pupil, Gabrielle Capet, are among the many women who followed Carriera's example to become successful pastel portraitists in the eighteenth century.

ANNE VALLAYER-COSTER (1744-1818)

Anne Vallayer-Coster was one of the most talented, versatile, and productive still life painters of the late eighteenth century. Within this genre she painted a wide variety of works, ranging from simple groups of humble kitchen objects to elaborate composi-tions of exotic things, as well as hunting trophies and arrangements of fruits. She was especially renowned for her paintings of bouquets of flowers.

Vallayer-Coster's technical skills were widely recognized and appreciated by her contemporaries. In 1771 the highly influential critic Diderot wrote that no other artist possessed an equal force of color and assurance. Among her patrons were the Marquis de Marigny, Minister of Arts under Louis XV, the Comte d'Angiviller, who held the same position under Louis XVI, and Marie Antoinette. Through royal de-cree, she was permitted to live in one of the apartments reserved for artists, a mark of special esteem that had also been accorded to Chardin, her more famous colleague who also specialized in still life painting. The official rewards and successes enjoyed by Vallayer-Coster during her lifetime attest to both the quality of her art and the es-teem in which naturalistic still life painting was held.

Anne Vallayer was born into a family of artisan-craftsmen. Her father was a goldsmith who worked for the Gobelins tapestry factory. Eventually, he established an independent shop which his wife ran after his death. Thus, Vallayer was raised in an environment that cultivated and encouraged her talents. We do not know how she acquired her painting skills, but she was an accomplished artist by her early twenties.

Vallayer's successful professional career enabled her to raise her social status. In 1781, at the relatively late age of 37, she married a wealthy lawyer and member of parliament, Jean Pierre Silvestre Coster, a match that represented a definite advance in class status for the daughter of a goldsmith.

Although Diderot was appreciative of Vallayer-Coster's talents, he was the first writer to compare her works with those of Chardin, and to some extent her reputation has suffered from this comparison ever since. One cannot deny that there are similarities in subjects and compositions between some of the still lifes of the two. However, one would find such constants in the works of almost any other eighteenth-century French still life painter. They are only the most general characteristics of national and period style in this specific type of painting. This does not indicate that Vallayer-Coster was less talented or less innovative than Chardin.

Similarities and differences between these two artists may be seen when one compares Vallayer-Coster's reception piece for the Academy, *Allegory of Music* (Figure 27) with Chardin's *Attributes of Music* (Figure 28). Both works depict a very similar selection of objects: musical instruments, music stand, sheet music, and a partially burnt candle. Submitting such an elaborate work as her reception piece indicates Vallayer-Coster's ambitious attempt to rival Chardin on the elevated level of a complex, allegorical still life.[3] Chardin placed his objects on a narrow ledge, parallel to the picture plane. There is no defined central focus and the objects appear casually jumbled on the table. In contrast, Vallayer-Coster's *Allegory of Music* is carefully composed with a clear diagonal movement from left to right. The lute, violin, and flute are linear elements that lead the viewer's eye back into space. This spatial recession is reinforced by the diagonal positioning of the table. As opposed to Chardin's random grouping, each object in Vallayer-Coster's painting has been selected and positioned to increase the compositional unity of the work and enhance its dynamic organizaton. Technically, Chardin is noted for his painterly surfaces, which suggest a variety of textures rather than describing them precisely. Vallayer-Coster's painting is executed in a controlled technique, without visible brushstrokes, which conveys a more precise description of the surfaces of objects.

Many of Vallayer-Coster's still lifes are not as elaborate as the *Allegory of*

FIGURE 27. ANNE VALLAYER-COSTER. *Allegory of Music.* 1770. Musée du Louvre, Paris.

FIGURE 28. JEAN-BAPTISTE CHARDIN. *Attributes of Music.* 1765. Oil on canvas. 35 13/16 x 57 1/16''. Musée du Louvre, Paris.

Music. She painted a number of works depicting simple objects set on a stone ledge. One of her most sensitive and beautiful still lifes of this type is *The White Soup Bowl* (Figure 29). This painting is a study in shades of white. The artist precisely and sensitively describes the different tones and textures of the porcelain bowl, the linen cloth, and the translucent steam rising from the soup. The composition is deceptively simple. There is a subtle play of horizontal, vertical, and diagonal linear accents that achieve a satisfying balance. The economy of the arrangement is consistent with the restrained color scheme of *The White Soup Bowl.* This painting displays a technical ability of extreme control and finesse. Furthermore, the image conveys tangibility and immediacy. The soup is steaming and soon someone will come to lift the ladle and serve the broth and bread to hungry people.

Vallayer-Coster's talents were not limited solely to the realm of still life painting. She also painted miniatures, portraits, and arrangements of fruits and flowers. Her paintings of flowers received widespread recognition and success, continuing the tradition of Peeters and Ruysch. Her flower compositions vibrate with color and freedom of touch, more characteristic of the nineteenth century than of the eighteenth. Both in flower paintings and still lifes, her precision and taste for reproducing exact detail served her purposes quite well. These talents were less appreciated in the realm of portraiture where, as noted in connection with Carriera's success in this field, the artist was expected to beautify the sitter's appearance as necessary.

Anne Vallayer-Coster was one of the finest French still life painters of her generation. She was a versatile artist with a sophisticated sense of composition and sen-

FIGURE 29. ANNE VALLAYER-COSTER. *The White Soup Bowl.* 1771. Oil on canvas. 19 11/16 x 24 1/2''. Private Collection.

sitivity to color combinations. Her paintings, like those of Chardin, are a realistic alternative to the erotic fantasies of the late Rococo painters, such as Boucher and Fragonard.

ELISABETH VIGÉE-LEBRUN (1755–1842)

Elisabeth Vigée-Lebrun was one of the finest and most successful aristocratic portrait painters of the late eighteenth and early nineteenth centuries. As official portraitist for Marie Antoinette, she achieved one of the highest positions in her society. After the French Revolution, as she traveled around Europe, she continued to experience a series of international triumphs. Her output was prodigious: She produced about 800 paintings during her lifetime. Like Carriera, to whom she was frequently compared by her contemporaries, Vigée-Lebrun had the capacity both to reflect and to formulate the esthetic tastes of her aristocratic clientele.

The daughter of a pastel portrait painter, Vigée-Lebrun recalled in her memoirs that her father and his colleagues gave her instruction and encouraged her talents. She also studied the paintings in the Louvre, especially Rubens' Marie de Medici cycle. In this active, supportive environment, her talents developed precociously. When she was twenty, she commanded higher prices for her portraits than any of her contemporaries.

In 1778 Vigée-Lebrun was summoned to court to paint her first portrait of Marie Antoinette. Thus began a relationship that would dominate the career and reputation of the artist. An ardent royalist until her death at the age of 87, Vigée-Lebrun was called upon to create the official image of the queen. The painting that best exemplifies Vigée-Lebrun's role as political propagandist is the monumental and complex *Marie Antoinette and Her Children* (Figure 30).[4] This work was commissioned directly from the funds of the state to defuse the violent attacks on the queen's moral character then circulating in France. It was painted only two years before the cataclysm of the French Revolution, the imprisonment of the royal family, and their subsequent execution. This official image was designed as an aggressive, if ultimately ineffective, counterattack to the political opponents of the monarchy. Vigée-Lebrun placed the queen in the imposing and easily recognizable setting of the Salon

FIGURE 30. ELISABETH VIGÉE-LEBRUN *Marie Antoinette and Her Children*. 1787. Musée National de Versailles.

de la Paix at Versailles. The famous Hall of Mirrors is visible on the left side of the painting. The royal crown sits on top of the cabinet on the right, the ultimate symbol of the power and authority of the kings. The figure of the queen herself dominates the composition. Her features have been ennobled and beautified, while the enormous hat and full, voluminous skirts create an impression of superhuman monumentality. Her luxuriant costume, the immense blue velvet robe and hat convey, like Rigaud's *Portrait of Louis XIV* (Figure 31) the grandeur of the French monarchy. Rigaud, however, relied on iconographical precedents. For his image of the Sun King, Rigaud adopted Louis XIV's stance from Van Dyck's *Portrait of Charles I*. Vigée-Lebrun wanted her painting to express not only the sanctity of divine right monarchy but also the bourgeois, Enlightenment concept of "Maternal Love." The triangular composition is derived from High Renaissance images of the Madonna and Child by Leonardo and Raphael. Like Kauffman's *Cornelia, Mother of the Gracchi* (see Figure 34), Marie Antoinette displays her children as her jewels. The Dauphin stands on the right, slightly apart from the group, as is only appropriate for the future king of France (although events were to alter the dynastic succession). The eldest daughter gazes up at the queen with filial adoration. It is traditionally believed that the empty cradle to

FIGURE 31. HYACINTHE RI-
GAUD. *Louis XIV*. 1701. Oil on
canvas. 9'2'' x 6'3''. Musée du
Louvre, Paris.

which the young Dauphin points originally contained the queen's fourth child, an infant girl, who died two months before the painting was to be exhibited at the Salon opening. On that day, August 25, 1787, anti-monarchist feelings were running so high that Vigée-Lebrun refused to display the painting for fear that it might be damaged.

There is a strong contrast between the opulent formality of *Marie Antoinette and Her Children* and Vigée-Lebrun's *Portrait of Hubert Robert* (Figure 32). Robert, a close friend of the artist, was a painter who specialized in the creation of picturesque classical ruins glowing in the rosy-tinted atmosphere invented by Claude Lorraine. As opposed to the formal reserve of Marie Antoinette, Robert leans casually on one arm. The relaxed pose contrasts with a tense, alert gaze. Robert seems to be receiving inspiration from some undetermined source. The sharp turn of the head, strong lighting, and sense of barely controlled energy convey a vivid sense of tangible presence. The face is painted realistically, which underscores the immediacy of the image. The

FIGURE 32. ELISABETH VIGÉE-LEBRUN. *Portrait of Hubert Robert.* 1788. Musée du Louvre, Paris.

barely restrained, proto-Romantic energy of Hubert Robert anticipates subsequent developments in romantic portraiture in the early nineteenth century.

Vigée-Lebrun positioned Robert against an undetailed, neutral background in which brushstrokes are visible. This plain ground is similar to those used by her colleague, Jacques Louis David, for portraits and other types of painting (see *Death of Marat*). However, the neutral background is in marked contrast to the bright, ruddy complexion of Robert and the three primary colors employed in his costume: a yellow vest, blue jacket, and red collar. The primary colors are echoed in the paint brushes, also tipped with red, yellow, and blue. The white cravat, which flows luxuriantly, is painted in impasto brushstrokes.

Her close association with the queen made it dangerous for Vigée-Lebrun to remain in France after the imprisonment of the royal family. In 1789 she traveled first to Italy, then Vienna, eventually arriving in St. Petersburg, Russia. There, no political

FIGURE 33. ELISABETH VIGÉE-LEBRUN. French, 1755–1842. *Varvara Ivanowna Nariskine, nee Ladomirsky, 1800.* Oil on canvas. 25 x 21 3/4''. Columbus Museum of Art, Ohio: Museum Purchase, Derby Fund.

revolution had dispersed the aristocratic clientele upon whom she depended for commissions.

The portrait of *Varvara Ivanova Narishkine* (Figure 33) was painted in Moscow in 1800. This strikingly beautiful Polish woman was the wife of a Russian prince. In this work, the sitter's hair is casually tied with a ribbon and cascades over one shoulder. She wears a simple red robe, in the antique style, over a white undergarment, parted to reveal a luscious bit of upper arm. The figure is placed before a sky-blue background. However, all details of costume and hair are subordinate to the beauty of this large-eyed young woman who gazes directly out at the viewer.

Vigée-Lebrun was permitted to return to Paris in 1802, in response to a petition signed by 255 fellow artists, but the era in which she had risen to fame had passed into history. She lived another forty years, sadly out of place in Napoleonic France and neglected during the subsequent Bourbon restoration.

Her career is of great historical interest because she was one of the foremost painters of her era. High prices, prestigious commissions, and critical attention document her position in the society of the *ancien régime*. Unlike David, who adapted his talents to the successive governments of France, Vigée-Lebrun was both emotionally and professionally attached to the monarchy. While the *Portrait of Marie Antoinette and Her Children* found a sympathetic audience during the restoration of the Bourbons at the Salon of 1817, its creator never regained the preeminent position she had held before Marie Antoinette was guillotined.

chapter 7

Neoclassical Painters and Sculptors

Neoclassicism was an international movement in the history of art that affected many artists between 1750 and 1850. During this epoch, both European and American painters and sculptors employed a formal vocabulary adapted from the art and artifacts of antiquity. Neoclassicism manifested itself in works of art in all media: painting, sculpture, and architecture, as well as designs for the decorative arts. Angelica Kauffman was one of the major painters in the first generation of neoclassical artists. The daughter of a Swiss artist, she worked in Italy and England as both a portrait painter for the aristocracy, like her contemporary Vigée-Lebrun, and as a creator of history paintings with didactic themes, drawn from ancient literature. During the third quarter of the nineteenth century, a group of American women sculptors established studios in Rome. Harriet Hosmer and Edmonia Lewis are among the artists who are known collectively as the ''White Marmorean Flock.'' This group set a historical precedent for the ability of women to become successful professional sculptors.

In Rome during the 1760s, a group of artists and scholars embraced the classical past as the only appropriate model for works of art. The German painter Anton Raphael Mengs, the Englishman Gavin Hamilton, and the American Benjamin West eagerly adapted didactic themes from ancient literature and depicted them in a classical style developed from contact with the surviving paintings and sculpture of antiquity. Angelica Kauffman played a significant role in the initial formulation of Neoclassicism and the dissemination of the style. Exposed to the circles in Rome that developed the theoretical principles of this movement, Kauffman traveled to England where she was received as a major artist who practiced both portraiture and history painting.

Neoclassicism retained its importance as an active style longer in sculpture than in painting. This is not surprising because styles in sculpture are generally slower to change than in painting. Furthermore, the art of antiquity had survived primarily in the medium of sculpture, and these classical models had rarely been seriously contested. During the first quarter of the nineteenth century, a number of Europeans, such as the Italian Antonio Canova and the Dane Bertel Thorwaldsen, were prominent sculptors in Rome who adapted a neoclassical style for their works, in conscious imitation of antique models.

When Horatio Greenough left America and traveled to Italy in 1825, he initiated the exodus that created the first significant American school of sculpture. Prior to this time, Americans who created three-dimensional objects were largely craftsmen, although Patience Lovell Wright (1725–1786) had been active as a maker of wax images in the eighteenth century. In addition to Greenough, Thomas Crawford and Hiram Powers are the most important neoclassical sculptors of the second quarter of the nineteenth century. Powers' *The Greek Slave* (see Figure 38) became the most famous sculpture produced by an American in the nineteenth century.

Italy retained its attraction for American sculptors during the third quarter of the nineteenth century. In addition to Randolph Rogers, William Wetmore Story, and William Henry Rinehart, a number of women sculptors established studios in Rome during the 1850s. The "White Marmorean Flock" created a series of famous and popular works, which, like those of their male colleagues, often combined classical subjects and forms with realistic details. American sculptors of both sexes were attracted to Italy for the same reasons. There they could study first-hand the sculpture of antiquity, which were accepted as models of excellence. The famous marble quarries of Carrara provided a ready source of materials. And, perhaps most important, there were many skilled artisans in Italy who could execute numerous replicas, enabling sculptors to fill commissions on demand. There are, for example, about thirty versions of Harriet Hosmer's *Puck*, one of which was owned by the Prince of Wales.

The largest collection of neoclassical sculpture ever assembled was exhibited at the Philadelphia Centennial Exposition in 1876. By this date, however, Neoclassicism was no longer a viable stylistic mode for American sculptors. Post-Civil War America, disillusioned with earlier ideals of America as the new Eden and absorbed in rapid industrialization, could no longer sustain a movement in scultpure that focused so resolutely on past models.

ANGELICA KAUFFMAN (1741–1807)

Like other artists discussed in preceding chapters, Angelica Kauffman was the daughter of a painter. Born in Switzerland, she received her early training from her Tyrolean father. During her childhood, the Kauffmans traveled about in Switzerland, Austria, and northern Italy, executing commissions for religious murals and portraits. Angelica's precocious talents were recognized and encouraged from an early age. In 1762 Angelica and her father arrived in Florence, and the following year they settled in Rome. Kauffman had the fortuitous opportunity to make contact with all the leading figures of the Neoclassical movement at a very early phase in its development.

Under the influence of Winckelmann, Mengs, and Hamilton, Kauffman developed a sophisticated neoclassical style that placed her in the forefront of this movement.

In 1766 Kauffman arrived in London where she quickly established herself as one of the leading artists of the English school. She became friendly with Sir Joshua Reynolds, and when the Royal Academy was founded in 1769, she and a flower painter, Mary Moser, were the only two women members. At this time, the vast majority of paintings produced in England were portraits commissioned by the aristocracy. Although she was forced to paint portraits to earn a steady income, Kauffman was one of the few artists working in England and one of the few women artists of any period who produced a steady stream of paintings with themes derived from classical and medieval history. Between 1766 and 1781, she contributed significantly to the widespread vogue for Neoclassicism in England.

In addition to the recognition she received for her history paintings, Kauffman's portraits were widely admired and she attracted many patrons among the English aristocracy. Her talents were held in such high esteem by her peers that she was asked to contribute to the decoration of the new residence of the Royal Academy in 1778.

Unfortunately, her professional successes were not matched by domestic happiness. In 1767 she married a man she believed to be a Swedish count but who turned out to be an imposter. After the scoundrel's death, she married a painter, Antonio Zucchi, who remained forever loyal and supportive of his more famous wife's career. In 1781, following their marriage, the couple returned to Italy. Refusing an offer to become resident court painter to the King of Naples, Kauffman settled in Rome in 1782. Some of her best paintings were created during these years.

Cornelia, Mother of the Gracchi (Figure 34) is one of the history paintings from her mature Roman period. Cornelia was a real matron in ancient Rome whose reputation as a paragon of virtue had come down through history. This painting illustrates a didactic anecdote in which a materialistic Roman woman, seated at the right, shows off a necklace, while Cornelia displays her three children as her "jewels." The stylized faces of the women, the severely simplified costumes, and the austere architecture are all characteristic of Kauffman's neoclassical style. The rich, glowing colors of the robes and the warm tonality of the light show her assimilation of the stylistic achievements of the Venetian school.

Cornelia is contemporary with David's *Oath of the Horatii* (Figure 35). A comparison between these two works reveals certain stylistic and compositional similarities as well as thematic differences. Both Kauffman and David arrange their figures in a simple, shallow space like a stage in a theater. Both use idealized classical figure types with legible gestures so the viewer can read the narrative. While both paintings depict an example of moral virtue, the virtues expressed are totally different in content. Cornelia is the admirable Roman matron who prizes her children above all worldly goods and devotes her life to raising them to serve the state. David focuses on the sacrifices of war, with emphasis clearly placed on the virile sons energetically dedicating their lives to defend the Roman Republic. While Kauffman has selected her didactic message to illustrate the behavior of a female role model, David's painting illustrates a male world of military heroism and patriotism. The women in the

FIGURE 34. ANGELICA KAUFFMAN, 1741–1807. *Cornelia Pointing to Her Children as Her Treasures.* Oil on canvas. 40 x 50''. Purchase: Williams Fund, 1975. Photo: #24155. Virginia Museum.

Oath of the Horatii are wilted, weak, limp, and tearful. They are clearly excluded from the male sphere and their role is confined to passive mourning.

Kauffman also combined a contemporary theme with art historical precedents to create her autobiographical image in *The Artist Hesitating Between the Arts of Music and Painting* (Figure 36). Here, Kauffman adapted the iconography of the story ''Hercules at the Crossroads between Fame and Luxury'' to illustrate an episode in her own youth when she had contemplated embarking on a career as an opera singer. This composition demonstrates the artist's ability to combine a specific portrait likeness (in this instance, a self-portrait) with the idealized neoclassical features of the two allegorical personifications. As Angelica gently presses the hand of Music on the left, her body inclines towards Painting, who points to the temple of fame, symbolically positioned on the summit of a distant mountain. As in *Cornelia, Mother of the Gracchi*, the drapery is painted in warm, glowing colors and the whole composition is bathed in a painterly atmosphere.

Kauffman's achievement places her in the forefront of Neoclassicism, as one of its original exponents and disseminators. By the 1760s she was creating convincing history paintings in a neoclassical idiom, anticipating David's paintings of the 1780s. She was one of the most highly respected artists of her era. Some measure of the admi-

FIGURE 35. JACQUES-LOUIS DAVID. *Oath of the Horatii*. 1784. Oil on canvas. Approx. 14' x 11'. Musée du Louvre, Paris.

ration and esteem she earned during her lifetime may be appreciated when one learns that all the members of the Roman Academy of St. Luke marched in her funeral procession. The funeral ceremonies were modeled after the services conducted for Raphael.

THE "WHITE MARMOREAN FLOCK"

In the mid-nineteenth century, a group of American women established studios in Rome and created a body of white marble sculpture that was often neoclassical in form and content. These artists were given the name "White Marmorean Flock" by the noted American novelist Henry James, and this quaint appellation is widely used today to identify these sculptors. Harriet Hosmer was one of the first women to settle in Rome, arriving in 1852. In the 1850s and 1860s, Louisa Lander, Emma Stebbins, Anne Whitney, and Edmonia Lewis established neighboring sculpture studios in Italy. These women were attracted to Rome for the same reasons as their male colleagues: the access to the famed statues of antiquity and the abundance of fine marble and of skilled artisans to work it. Furthermore, they also found in Rome an interna-

FIGURE 36. ANGELICA KAUFFMAN. *The Artist Hesitating Between the Arts of Music and Painting.* c. 1794. Lord St. Oswald, Nostell Priory, England.

tional community of artists who respected their unusual choice of profession. In Italy, members of the "Flock" were released from the cultural restrictions imposed on women by American Victorian society. This freedom, combined with inexpensive living costs, made Rome especially attractive to these American sculptors.

Harriet Hosmer (1830–1908)

The best known figure of the White Marmorean Flock is Harriet Hosmer, who initiated her training in America. She studied anatomy at the Saint Louis Medical College, following the same course as Hiram Powers. Hosmer's most famous statue is *Zenobia in Chains* (Figure 37), depicting the queen of Palmyra who was marched in chains through the streets of Rome following the defeat of her army in 272 A.D. Hosmer does not present Zenobia as a powerful warrior who, according to the historian Gibbon, conquered Egypt and parts of Asia Minor, but rather as a noble captive who accepts her defeat with dignity and reserve. Clothed in a Greek peplos, Zenobia stands ready to accept her fate. Like Cornelia, Zenobia was a woman of outstanding talents and abilities whose reputation survived through history and made her a female role model from the classical past. The selection of Zenobia was a deliberate choice by Hosmer. A contemporary writer in a letter to the *Boston Transcript* stated that it was Zenobia's "womanly modesty, her manly courage, and her intellectual tastes," that first attracted Hosmer. Knowing how

FIGURE 37. HARRIET HOS-
MER. *Zenobia in Chains*. 1859.
Marble. H.: 49''. Courtesy Wads-
worth Atheneum, Hartford.

much Hosmer admired Zenobia's qualities, it is valid to view this work as an
idealized model for contemporary women. The original statue, 7 feet tall, presented
a regally grand woman "fettered, yet proud and courageous."[1]

A comparison of Hosmer's *Zenobia* with Powers' *The Greek Slave* (Figure
38) reveals interesting differences in attitude toward the portrayal of the female
image that existed between two artists of the same neoclassical movement, one a
man, the other a woman. Powers made *The Greek Slave*'s nudity acceptable to
prudish Victorian American society by the literary references surrounding the work.
On one level, the figure was meant to evoke pity rather than lust, since she has
been captured by the Turks during the Greek War of Independence. She is naked
because she is about to be sold into slavery. But this motif was merely a respectable
pretext because the statue is clearly designed to titillate the Victorian male viewer,
and the chains emphasize the captive's passivity and vulnerability. By contrast,
Zenobia, although chained, is clothed and retains her dignity and integrity as a
woman. In this work, Hosmer provided an alternative to the sexual objectification
of women so evident in *The Greek Slave* and chose, instead, to depict an individual
woman of antiquity, worthy of deep respect and admiration on a number of levels.

Hosmer created another impressive image of a heroine in her statue *Beatrice*

FIGURE 38. HIRAM POWERS, 1805–1873. *The Greek Slave.*
1847. Marble. H.: 65 1/2''. Gift of Franklin Murphy, Jr., 1926.
Photographer: Armen, February 1972. Collection of the Newark
Museum.

Cenci (Figure 39), which has been described as "a moving, expressive figure and
one of the most successful reclining sculptures of the Neoclassical movement."[2]
Cenci was executed in 1599 for her participation in the murder of her cruel, evil
father. This story had inspired a series of works of art beginning in the Baroque
era. In the nineteenth century, the romantic poet Shelley wrote a verse drama based
on the episode that glorified the tyrannicide.

Hosmer's elegant and graceful statue is one of the most beautiful creations
by an American neoclassical sculptor. The soft folds of drapery and the sensuality
of her exposed body are contrasted with the hard stone slab upon which Beatrice
Cenci reclines. The drapery folds are much more fluid than Zenobia's, and Cenci's
face conveys an idealized prettiness that contrasts with Zenobia's heavier, more
classical features. The gentle arch of the figure's body creates a pleasant and active

FIGURE 39. HARRIET HOSMER. *Beatrice Cenci*. 1853–55. Marble. The Mercantile Library of St. Louis. St. Louis, Missouri.

contour. Hosmer depicts Beatrice Cenci asleep, but her sleep implies her impending doom.

Edmonia Lewis (1843–ca. 1900)

One of the most interesting artists in the Flock was Edmonia Lewis, who was half black and half Indian. The subjects of her sculpture reflect her racial heritage. In 1867, as a monument to the recent emancipation of the American slaves, Lewis created a two-figure group, *Forever Free*. The white marble sculpture presents a black woman kneeling in a gesture of prayer beside a standing black man who displays his broken chains.

Lewis was raised as a Chippewa Indian. *The Old Indian Arrowmaker and His Daughter* (Figure 40) is one example of her ability to create sculptural images of Indians of great dignity and symbolic force. This work contains some very realistic details. Object textures of the fur garments are articulated, and the Old Arrowmaker has a sharply defined face with prominent cheekbones. The presence of realistic details in works by neoclassical sculptors was very common. For example,

FIGURE 40. EDMONIA LEWIS. *Old Indian Arrowmaker and His Daughter*. 1872. George Washington Carver Museum, Tuskegee Institute.

FIGURE 41. ANTONIO CANOVA. *Maria Paulina Borghese, as Venus*. 1808. Marble. 62⅞ x 78¾″ (including bed). Galleria Borghese, Rome. Photograph by David Finn from *Canova* published by Abbeville Press, 1983, New York.

Canova's *Pauline Borghese as Venus* (Figure 41) combines a highly idealized body with a more specific portrait likeness in the head and precise textures of the couch on which the figure reclines. Thus, both Canova and Lewis combine realistic details with elements of the ideal, utilizing them at will as alternative modes.

The achievements of the sculptors of the "Marmorean Flock" were widely recognized in their era, and many of these women received commissions for monumental works to be placed outdoors. Although in retrospect their works may seem stylistically conservative, this should not affect our appreciation of the historical position and achievement of these artists. Their statues were highly regarded in their day and were extremely popular. The works of the Flock embodied an idealism and optimism that reflected American aspirations and expectations of the mid-nineteenth century. The critical success and widespread recognition of this group is significant not only historically but also because it set a precedent for the many important women sculptors of the twentieth century.

chapter 8

Introduction
to the Modern Era

The beginnings of the modern world are generally traced to the late eighteenth century when two types of revolutions began to transform European and American society. The Industrial Revolution and the American and French revolutions affected women differently from the ways in which they affected men. The immediate effects of the French Revolution transformed women's political and legal rights less than the economic changes brought about by the Industrial Revolution. Changes in infant mortality rates and family size, as well as the spread of public education, also had a profound impact on the patterns of women's lives during the nineteenth century. The feminist movement, active after the mid-nineteenth century, eventually succeeded in obtaining the expanded political and legal rights enjoyed by women in the twentieth century. The modern world has seen a slow but constant progression toward equality between the sexes, although discrimination toward women has not been eliminated.

By the mid-nineteenth century, most women married over the age of 20. French women married somewhat earlier than their British counterparts, but they restricted family size so they could reenter the labor force. Infant mortality rates dropped dramatically in the early twentieth century, as did the average number of births. The desire to improve one's socioeconomic position also affected the size of families. With fewer children to support, family resources could be channeled to permit upward mobility. The continued improvements in care for mothers and the decrease in infant mortality rates altered older patterns. Contemporary women are much less physically threatened by their role as childbearers. However, the emotional demands of motherhood grew as the birth rate decreased.

> Fewer children with longer lives entailed stronger emotional commitment to each one and heightened concern for the quality of child care. Expert opinion converged to professionalize motherhood. Thus while some forces freed women from the endless cycle of childbearing, traditionalism crept in by another door in another guise.[1]

WORKING WOMEN AND THE
INDUSTRIAL REVOLUTION

Recent studies indicate that early industrialization did not dramatically influence the types of work women performed. "The majority of women remained in household settings as family farm workers, shopkeepers and servants in France, as servants in Britain, as garment workers and casual laborers in both countries."[2] Throughout the nineteenth century women continued to perform low-skilled jobs with low productivity and low pay. This trend continued until World War I. In 1911, over 70 percent of English working women were either servants, textile workers, or garment workers. The vast majority of women workers were young and single. This group provided the pool from which employers hired women for work in textile factories and other industries. By 1851, in France, for example, women constituted 39 percent of the industrial labor force. This high percentage of women is explained by the fact that women worked for about one-half the wages of men.

While factory work provided regular, year-round employment, most female industrial workers toiled in miserable conditions for long hours at below-subsistence levels of pay. One reason women's wages remained so low was that women were generally unskilled workers. Unions restricted the numbers of women who could work in the better paying, more highly skilled jobs in the industrial sector. Few women underwent technical training. Only after the beginning of World War I, when so many men were called to fight the war, did women begin to enter the skilled trades.

Social legislation began to set limits on the number of hours and conditions of work for women and children. Beginning in England in 1841, and in 1874 in France, the work day was eventually shortened from 12 to 10 hours. As opposed to starting to work at age 6, girls were not permitted to work until age 13 or 14. Increasingly, married women without the skills to earn high wages relied on their husbands to be the primary wage earners. Because work was now located outside the home, it was more difficult for lower-class women to combine child rearing with employment for wages. "By 1900 the separation between home and work which had begun a century before was virtually complete."[3] This pattern of women's work continued into the twentieth century. Married women worked less often and only in response to the family's needs. The primary occupation of a married woman was that of wife and mother.

Around 1900 there was a shift from factory work to white-collar employment. Women began to be hired in sales, clerical positions, and the like, which demanded at least a rudimentary education. A small minority of working-class women became teachers and nurses.

Between the two world wars, more and more women worked in the "service" sectors: behind counters and cash registers, as social workers, nurses, and teachers. Many women who had previously been employed in the agricultural sector moved to cities. The rural exodus was widespread. Urban working opportunities offered better wages and regulation of working conditions. Since World War II, the ability of women to earn wages has contributed to the trend toward increased autonomy and freedom from the authority of the husband. The large proportion of women in the work force today may also be attributed to improved household technology, as well as declining birth rates and longer life spans. As Kessler-Harris notes: "Working women, as a group, are becoming older, better educated, less likely to take time off for babies and more likely to be married and have children."[4] However, discriminatory hiring and pay has limited women's financial independence and full equality in contemporary society.

WOMEN'S RIGHTS AND THE
FEMINIST MOVEMENT

The Enlightenment thinkers of the mid-eighteenth century did not present a clear case for the legal and professional equality of women. However, Montesquieu and Voltaire did formulate arguments in favor of increased educational opportunities for women. These thinkers countered the prevailing notions of women's intellectual inferiority. The *philosophes* believed that upper-class women should be able to use their skills and education more constructively in the world. Rousseau, however, the most influential Enlightenment thinker, extolled the new bourgeois concept of the family as a closely knit emotional unit. For women, marriage and motherhood were the expected sources of personal happiness. The woman's world was limited to her home. This glorification of woman as wife and mother was accompanied by the ideal conception of the home as a safe haven from the harsh realities of the world.[5] With the growing numbers of the middle classes during the nineteenth century, more and more women were affected by this life option. Any woman whose husband provided an adequate income was expected to find personal happiness in fulfilling her duties as wife and mother. For the middle-class woman, professional work was forbidden. As noted above, this bourgeois ideal of the role of the married woman as wife and mother affected the lower classes by the early twentieth century.

The French Revolution extended legal rights and privileges to many more men than had previously enjoyed them, but it left women largely unaffected. Women remained perpetual legal minors. Despite this, women did make some gains toward improved rights during these upheavals. Marriage was deemed a civil contract. Women won legal protection for their property and inheritance rights. A leading champion of equality of education for women was the Marquis de Condorcet. Inspired by the American Declaration of Independence, Condorcet demanded increased educational and social opportunities for women as well as civil equality. In fact, the National Convention passed laws in 1794 and 1795 providing free and compulsory education for girls as well as boys. Unfortunately, the instability of the time prevented the implementation of these plans. The Napoleonic Code of 1804 reversed any gains women may have achieved. The Code strengthened the patriarchal authority of the husband and father, inspired by the Roman model of the *pater familias*. The right to divorce was abolished in 1815, not to be reinstated until 1884. When a French woman married, she forfeited virtually all of her legal rights:

The law . . . required the wife to obey the husband, in return for which the husband owed her "protection." She had to reside wherever he chose and he was entitled to use force to compel her to do so. If she committed adultery, she was liable to imprisonment for a period of between three and twenty-four months, but he could engage in it with impunity. . . . She could not go to law without his permission even if she had her own business and she could not sell or buy without his approval. . . . The husband had the sole right to administer the joint estate. . . . He had full powers over his children, but when he died, she must act with the consent of his two nearest relatives.[6]

In colonial America, the general shortages of labor in general and women in particular gave women a higher status than in Europe. Most women married, and the scarcity of women may have resulted in greater social mobility. Colonial women worked in a wide variety of occupations both inside and outside of the home. Women published and printed newspapers, managed tanneries, and worked, it seems, in almost every occupation in the Colonies. Unlike their European counterparts, they were allowed to conduct financial transactions and were often named as executors of their husband's estates.

Early nineteenth-century women in America were idealized as the guardians of traditional moral values. Many women were active in the Abolitionist and temperance movements. From this background, the movement for women's rights was born in 1848 at the Seneca Falls Convention, organized by Lucretia Mott, a Quaker, and Elizabeth Cady Stanton. A *Declaration of Principles,* which paraphrased the Declaration of Independence, included a resolution for women's suffrage. Through the second half of the nineteenth century, the suffrage movement, which also fought for equal legal rights, equal pay for equal work, and access to education, began to gain momentum. In 1888, the International Council of Women held their founding convention in Washington, D.C.

Despite growing involvement of large numbers of women in the suffrage movement, especially in America and Britain, it was only as a result of World War I that women were enfranchised. This occurred in Austria, Canada, Denmark, Germany, Great Britain, the Netherlands, Russia, Sweden, the United States, and in other countries. French women did not win the right to vote until 1944.

In addition to legal and civil discrimination, women were also prevented from developing other options in their lives by the restrictions imposed on their educational and professional training. Lower-class women received virtually no education. In France, only after 1850 were towns required to provide primary education for girls. Middle- and upper-class women received a rudimentary education either in convent schools or with tutors in the home. As in the Renaissance, a woman's education tended to reinforce her predetermined life roles as wife and mother, rather than providing practical skills that might lead to financial self-sufficiency. Instruction in drawing and water-color painting was part of this bourgeois curriculum because "Art" was considered an appropriate hobby for women, if forbidden as a professional career. Women slowly began to enter universities and professional schools, including the art academies, after 1850.

In America, opportunities for education were similar to those in Europe during the eighteenth century. However, American women had access to education earlier than in Europe. Public education for both boys and girls was a priority for the new democracy. Many teachers willing to work for modest salaries were needed, and teaching became one of the few appropriate professions for women. To train these teachers, a few private colleges for women were opened from 1850. Through the 1890s, teaching was the main occupation of female college graduates.

Slowly, during the second half of the nineteenth century, a few women entered European universities. In France, the first woman enrolled in medical school in 1868; the law faculty admitted its first woman in 1884. University education remained a potential option for a tiny percentage of women throughout this period.

The general tendency for women to be excluded from professional careers of all types explains the low absolute numbers of professional women artists at the beginning of the nineteenth century. However, during the course of the century, more and more women (as well as men) became practicing artists. By 1900 thousands of women all over Europe were regularly displaying their works in official exhibitions. In the French Salon of 1801, 28 women participated. By 1878, 762 women were exhibiting. With increasing numbers of competent professionals, it is not surprising to find a larger number of women artists achieving excellence and working in the avant-garde movements of the art world. Since the 1870s, women artists have been active in almost every major avant-garde movement.

During the twentieth century, the numbers of practicing professional women artists have risen dramatically, and the trend continues unabated. In 1972, 75 percent of all the art students in America were women. Today, the aspiring young woman artist can receive a thorough artistic training, completely equivalent to that available to men. Of course, the more subtle obstacles of cultural conditioning and societal expectations have proven difficult to eliminate. In 1972, a maximum of ten percent of all works of art purchased by museums were created by women, and only 18 percent of all commercial galleries exhibited any works by women.

As one might expect from the increased absolute numbers of women artists and the enlarged opportunities to receive professional training, women artists have played a more important role in the history of art of the twentieth century than in earlier periods. This will be immediately apparent from the number of artists discussed in the chapters that follow.

chapter 9

Painters in France: 1850–1900

During the second half of the nineteenth century, more and more women in Europe became practicing professional artists. One explanation for this phenomenon was the acknowledged surplus of unmarried women among the bourgeoisie. A career in the arts, like teaching, was one of the few acceptable means for a middle-class spinster to earn her living. These women were active in both the fine arts of painting and sculpture (to a lesser degree), as well as in the crafts traditionally associated with women, such as embroidery, lacemaking, china painting, and book illustration.

Another reason more women turned to art was the increased access to training, in public and private schools and artists' studios, during the nineteenth century, although women's art education still remained discriminatory. In 1790 Adelaide Labille-Guiard, a noted portrait painter and contemporary of Vigée-Lebrun, submitted a report to the Franch National Assembly outlining a model curriculum to train indigent women for employment in the industries of the ''decorative'' or ''applied arts.'' In 1805 the first free drawing school for women was founded in Paris. In 1849, after the death of her father, Rosa Bonheur assumed the directorship of this school. By 1879 there were 20 such schools in Paris solely designed to train women for positions in the art industries, although such jobs were scarce and underpaid. In the first half of the nineteenth century, women could also study privately in the studios of established artists. During the 1870s there was a separate women's class at alternative schools such as the Académie Julian in Paris, where women worked with a model. In 1896 the most prestigious art academy of France, the Ecole des Beaux-Arts, officially admitted women, thus removing the most obvious institutional barrier to equality of artistic training. This feminist victory was achieved only after seven years of sustained political pressure by the Union des Femmes Peintres et Sculpteurs, the first professional organization of women artists in France.[1]

In Germany an equivalent group, the Verein der Kunstlerinnen, had been founded in 1869. This society established separate schools in Berlin and Munich to train women artists. As late as the 1890s, women were still not permitted to study at the state-sponsored art academies in Germany or Austria. The Royal Academy in London admitted its first woman in 1861, but a life drawing class was not provided for women until 1893. It is interesting that in America women achieved more equality of opportunity for artistic training earlier than in Europe. At the Pennsylvania Academy of Fine Arts, women could draw from plaster casts as early as 1844. By 1860, women were enrolled in the anatomy class, and a separate life drawing class was established for women in 1868.[2]

Of the four artists to be discussed in this chapter, only Rosa Bonheur was the daughter of an artist. Berthe Morisot, Mary Cassatt, and Paula Modersohn-Becker all benefited directly from the increased access to professional artistic training that became available, at least for middle-class women, in the second half of the nineteenth century.

Rosa Bonheur painted images of animals in naturalistic landscapes with scientific accuracy and a fidelity to direct observation characteristic of the movement known as Realism. The Realists "sought to revitalize the centuries-old artistic tradition of accurate, truthful recording of the world and to give this tradition contemporary relevance."[3] Typical examples of the Realists' interest in ordinary people in everyday environments can be seen in Honoré Daumier's *The Third-Class Carriage* (ca. 1862) and Gustave Courbet's *Stonebreakers* (1849). Among the many artists who participated in Realism during the 1860s are Camille Corot, Jean-François Millet, and Edouard Manet.

Although a few women artists had been stylistically innovative in the past, Impressionism is the first avant-garde movement in the history of art in which women were significant members. Both Berthe Morisot and Mary Cassatt exhibited with the group and maintained strong personal and professional ties with the male Impressionist painters. However, despite the close association of Cassatt with Degas, and Morisot with Manet and Renoir, each of these women developed an individual and original painting style that was certainly equal in quality to that of their more famous male colleagues.

Like the Norwegian Edvard Munch, the Spaniard Pablo Picasso, and the American Mary Cassatt, Paula Modersohn-Becker was a non-French artist whose career was decisively influenced by exposure to the Parisian avant-garde at a formative phase in her development. Modersohn-Becker was the first artist from Germany to evolve a personal post-impressionist style based on a synthesis of German and French influences. She created images that are symbols of the enduring life force of the human race.

ROSA BONHEUR (1822–1899)

Rosa Bonheur was one of the most famous and popular French painters of her epoch. She devoted her entire career to painting animals, both domesticated and wild, in outdoor settings. Her style was based on a complete dedication to precise observation and the thorough study of animal anatomy characteristic of Realism. Many Romantic artists, such as Eugène Delacroix, Antoine-Louis Barye, and George Stubbs, chose to depict violent attacks of predatory animals when they selected subjects from the animal realm. Bonheur, by contrast, avoided bloody encounters between animals, preferring more peaceful situations that she could observe directly. Her innovative animal subjects, depicted with naturalism of detail, were greatly appreciated by her contemporaries. Numerous engravings, after her compositions, were circulated in Europe and America, ensuring her widespread popularity and fame. Bonheur has the distinction of being the first woman artist to be honored with the highest award of the French government, the Cross of the Legion of Honor. The empress of France presented the medal to Bonheur in her studio in 1865.

Born in Bordeaux, Bonheur received her initial training, along with the other children of the family, from her father. All four Bonheur siblings became competent *animaliers*, i.e., artists who specialized in animal subjects. She is the first woman artist in the nineteenth century whose upbringing was directly affected by the feminism of the utopian philosophical movement known as St. Simonianism. Bonheur's father, Raymond, was an active member of the St. Simonians, who believed that both women and artists had special roles to play in the creation of the future perfect society. The St. Simonians prayed to "God, Father and Mother of us all." Late in her life, Bonheur told her biographer:

> Why would I not be proud to be a woman? My father . . . told me many times that the mission of women was to elevate the human race, to be the Messiah of future centuries. I owe to these doctrines the great and proud ambition I maintain for the sex to which I have the honor to belong. . . . I am certain that to us belongs the future. . . .[4]

While women gained a much higher status in this ideal, utopian community, it was assumed that the leaders of the group would be male. One can understand Raymond Bonheur's attraction to St. Simonianism since male artists were given an important leadership role: "It was taught that the religious side of the sect would be directed by the man of the most artistic nature, who would be the supreme priest."[5] Armed from childhood with a belief in the innate superiority and religious mission of both women and artists to transform society, Bonheur developed her talents to the fullest extent possible. Her dedication to her art was total and unequivocal.

Bonheur was a fiercely independent and unusual individual who exhibited courageous nonconformity. Unlike Cassatt and Morisot, she did not accept many of her society's conventions for women's behavior. For example, she obtained official permission in 1852 to wear men's clothing so she could move about with freedom to study animal anatomy in the slaughterhouses of Paris or in the markets where live animals were sold. She never married but lived for over forty years with a female companion, Natalie Micas. After 1853 she did not exhibit her paintings at the Salons. She could maintain her financial independence from the proceeds of private sales and the income produced from engravings of her compositions.

Although Bonheur acquired the rudimentary principles of painting from her father, the true basis upon which she built her images came from her studies of animal anatomy. A Realist urge toward accuracy is clearly apparent in Bonheur's masterpiece *The Horse Fair* (Figure 42). This large painting (over 16 feet wide) won immediate critical and popular acclaim for its creator, firmly establishing her reputation. It attracted large crowds when it was displayed in France, England, and America. Widely reproduced in engravings, this work became one of the most famous paintings of the nineteenth century. Bonheur said that *The Horse Fair* was originally inspired by the frieze of horsemen on the Parthenon. The even distribution of the horses across the picture surface and the processional movement from left to right do recall the Parthenon frieze (Figure 43). One can also see an echo of a Parthenon horseman in the man with an upraised arm, riding the rearing black horse in the center of the composition. However, instead of the classical restraint, simplicity, and slowly measured pace of the Parthenon frieze, Bonheur has presented an image of forceful energy, in which men and horses strain against one another. Another interesting comparison may be made with a painting by Theodore Gericault, whom she admired. Bonheur manages to endow her image with the same romantic spirit and energy that Gericault gave both his horse and rider in *Mounted Officer of the Imperial Guard* (1812).

In actuality, *The Horse Fair* is also the result of a conscientious study of horses at a market that was located on the outskirts of Paris. Both the realism of details, the large scale, and the unified composition contribute to the powerful impression the work makes on the viewer. Bonheur has designed an unprecedented scene of great excitement, vividly portrayed, which places the viewer in the midst of the action as the horses are displayed in a circle.

FIGURE 42.   MARIE ROSA BONHEUR, 1882–1899. *Horse Fair*. Oil on canvas. H.: 96 1/4'', W.: 199 1/2''. Signed and dated lower right Rosa Bonheur 1853–5. The Metropolitan Museum of Art, Gift of Cornelius Vanderbilt, 1887. All rights reserved, The Metropolitan Museum of Art.

FIGURE 43.   Horsemen, from the west frieze of the Parthenon. c. 440 B.C.
Marble. H.: 43''. British Museum, London. Reproduced by courtesy of
the Trustees of the British Museum.

After 1860 Bonheur lived with Natalie Micas in relative isolation near Fontainebleau, where she continuously studied the natural beauty of the forest and surrounding farms. On the extensive grounds of her chateau, she kept a personal menagerie to permit her to observe a variety of animals. *On the Alert* (Figure 44) is a characteristic example of her later paintings. Here one can see the dignity and respect she brought to the study of animals. Her empathy with animals was very intense: She often referred to them as her ''friends.'' In this closely studied ''portrait,'' one can sense an almost human quality of communication in the expressive gaze of the noble stag.

Bonheur remained faithful to her form of realism throughout her life, keeping her vision fresh and direct in all her works. Her intense powers of observation and her humility before the wonders of nature impressed her contemporaries, who frequently compared her art to the Dutch painters of the seventeenth century who set the standards for realistic description.

BERTHE MORISOT (1841–1895)

Although increasing numbers of women artists employed conservative painting styles in the nineteenth century, Berthe Morisot has the distinction of having been one of the founding members of the avant-garde group known as the Impressionists. Like the other members of the group, Morisot devoted her career to the creation of images that

FIGURE 44. ROSA BONHEUR. *On the Alert.* 1878.
Present whereabouts unknown.

depict, with elegance and spontaneity, intimate scenes from daily life. Often using
her family as models, Morisot's paintings permit the viewer to enter a closed domestic
realm populated mainly by women and children.

Morisot's art is characterized by delicate brushwork and elegant colors, juxtaposed in subtle harmonies. These ''feminine'' qualities of her paintings were regularly noted by critics evaluating her works. In a hostile review of the Impressionist
exhibition of 1875, one critic wrote of her paintings: ''. . . feminine grace is preserved amidst the frenzy of a mind in delirium.''[6] However, Morisot's art is not more
or less ''feminine'' than many of the paintings of her ''masculine'' colleagues. Impressionist paintings regularly employed delicate colors, obvious brushwork, and
domestic subjects.

Morisot was born in Bourges into an upper-middle class family. When she was
seven, the family moved to Paris. She and her sister, Edma, were given drawing lessons at an early age. Both sisters showed greater dedication to their art than was ex-

pected from or appropriate for women of their class. One of their teachers, Joseph Alexandre Guichard, warned Mme. Morisot:

> Considering the characters of your daughters, my teaching will not endow them with minor drawing room accomplishments; they will become painters. Do you realize what this means? In the upper class milieu to which you belong, this will be revolutionary, I might almost say catastrophic. Are you sure that you will not come to curse the day when art, having gained admission to your home, now so respectable and peaceful, will become the sole arbiter of the fate of two of your children?[7]

In 1861 the Morisot sisters met Camille Corot, who became their mentor for the next five years. Berthe Morisot's early paintings reveal Corot's influence in the rendition of effects of early morning light and in the closely toned color harmonies in her landscapes.

In 1868 Morisot met Edouard Manet and, through him, most of the members of the Impressionist group. Morisot encouraged Manet to take up painting outdoors. In 1874 she married his younger brother Eugène Manet. Although Edma stopped painting after her marriage, Berthe pursued her career throughout her lifetime, with only a brief interruption for the birth of her daughter.

The Cradle (Figure 45), a beautiful and characteristic example of Morisot's Impressionist style, depicts her sister Edma gazing tenderly at her newborn child. This is an intimate, domestic moment that turns the viewer into either a member of the family circle or an interloper. The image is a study in tonalities. The translucent, pearly-gray of the fabric covering the cradle is highlighted with a few touches of pure white. The drapery covering the window is suffused with a blue hue indicating filtered daylight. The overall touch is quite painterly and the baby is indicated with the barest economy.

Another work by Morisot, *On the Balcony* (Figure 46), demonstrates the artist's interest in the integration of figure and landscape within a unifying exterior atmosphere. In this way, *On the Balcony* is typical of such Impressionist works as Renoir's *Le Moulin de la Galette*, which also depicts contemporary people illuminated by a specific yet natural light source.

A comparison between Morisot's *On the Balcony* and a painting of Manet's from the following year, *Mother and Child, Gare Saint-Lazare* (Figure 47), reveals major differences in the styles of these two artists. While both works depict a mother and daughter seen from behind, positioned against a railing, there are few additional similarities. Morisot's mother leans protectively over her child; they are united emotionally. Manet's pair, by contrast, appear distanced and unrelated. Morisot concentrates on the creation of a specific effect of light, while Manet's image is more crystalline, with clearly defined contours and firmly modeled forms. Manet's technique is more linearly precise while Morisot's touch reveals a greater degree of Impressionist spontaneity.

In the 1880s Morisot's brushwork took on even greater fluidity and energy, sometimes with only partial success. During the following decade, under the influence of Renoir, she painted with long, flowing brushstrokes in which highly saturated

FIGURE 45.   BERTHE MORISOT. *The Cradle*. 1872. 22 1/2
x 18 1/2''. Paris, Musée d'Orsay, Galerie du Jeu de Paume.

colors maintain the contours of the figures. It is generally accepted that her works
from the 1870s, when the Impressionist movement was at its height, are her finest
paintings.

As a full-fledged member of the Impressionist group, Berthe Morisot occupies
a secure position in the history of art. United by common interests with the Impressionists, Morisot developed a personal style of originality, fluidity, and delicacy.
Along with her male colleagues and Cassatt, these artists valued the private women's
world of home and family and created pleasantly delightful images of beauty and elegance.

MARY CASSATT (1844–1926)

Like Berthe Morisot, Mary Cassatt was an active and loyal member of the Impressionist group. Born in Pittsburgh into an upper-middle class family similar in status to

FIGURE 46. BERTHE MORISOT. *On the Balcony*. 1872. 23 1/2 x 19''. Present whereabouts unknown.

Morisot's, Cassatt also possessed the personal strength and force of her convictions to pursue a career as an avant-garde painter, eschewing official recognition and juried competitions. Stimulated by the exciting environment of Paris, Cassatt became, in the view of many scholars, the best American artist, male or female, of her generation.

Cassatt overrode her family's initial resistance to her early decision to become an artist. In 1861 she entered the Pennsylvania Academy of Fine Arts, one of the first art academies in the world to open its doors to women. After four years of study there, she recognized the limitations that America imposed on artists. Like the women of the "White Marmorean Flock" and many male artists of her generation, she traveled to Europe in the late 1860s to study the old masters. After 1872 she settled permanently in Paris and pursued her artistic training. Here her sister Lydia and her parents joined her in 1877. Although she became most famous for her paintings of mothers and children, Cassatt never married. She continued to paint until the age of 70 when her eyesight began to fail. Her achievement was recognized, relatively late in her life, by the award of the medal of the French Legion of Honor in 1904.

FIGURE 47. EDOUARD MANET. French, 1832–1883. *Gare Saint-Lazare*. Dated 1873. Canvas, 0.933 x 1.145 (36 3/4 x 45 1/8"). National Gallery of Art, Washington. Gift of Horace Havemeyer in memory of his mother, Louisine W. Havemeyer, 1956.

Cassatt possessed a brilliant instinct for determining what the history of art has deemed most important in the confusingly active art world of Paris. She told her biographer that, by the late 1870s, when Degas invited her to participate in the Impressionist exhibitions, "I had already recognized who were my true masters. I admired Manet, Courbet and Degas. I hated conventional art. I began to live."[8] Cassatt learned from these artists without losing her individuality and personal style.

In the late 1870s and 1880s, Cassatt's works reflect the influence of Impressionism. *The Loge* (Figure 48), a painting of the artist's sister Lydia, was exhibited in the fourth Impressionist exhibition of 1879 and is characteristic of Impressionism in a number of ways. Degas and Renoir had previously painted women at the opera, so the subject is typical of the Impressionists' taste for scenes of the amusements of Parisian life. The relaxed asymmetrical pose of the sitter, with one arm cropped by the picture frame, is also a typical Impressionist device. Degas would often "cut" his figures to convey a sense of immediacy, almost like a snapshot photo. In this painting, Cassatt was extremely interested in the effects of artifical light on flesh tones. Like Degas' studies of ballerinas on the stage, also illuminated by artifical gas lights, Lydia's face and shoulders are unnaturally radiant. Despite these glowing effects of artificial light,

FIGURE 48.   MARY CASSATT. *In the Loge*. 1879. Oil
on canvas. 31 5/8 x 23''. Philadelphia Museum of Art: Bequest of Charles Dorrance Wright (1978–1–5).

the figure is firmly modeled and her contours are well defined. Brushstrokes are evident in Lydia's dress, fan, and the reflected background. The spontaneity of Cassatt's
touch is another element that connects her style with Impressionism. *The Loge* is
painted with a sophisticated and original color sensibility. The pink dress is beautifully contrasted with the ruby-red banquette. The colors shimmer and sparkle in the
gas light of the theater at intermission. An innovative aspect of this work is the use of a
mirrored background. This device conveys a reflection of the space, in which the
viewer must also sit, without creating an actual illusion or description of deep space.
Thus, the picture includes an image of the environment of the opera without violating
the flat, two-dimensionality of the picture surface. Cassatt's use of a mirrored background anticipates Manet's similar use of a mirror in his famous work, *The Bar at the
Folies-Bergères* (1881–82).

Beginning in the late 1880s, the works of Cassatt and many other Impressionists
demonstrate a renewed concern with the clear articulation of forms. Obvious

brushstrokes are eliminated, colors become more highly saturated and less naturalistic, and compositions develop greater structure. These post-Impressionist qualities are all clearly apparent in one of Cassatt's largest and most ambitious paintings, *The Boating Party* (Figure 49). In this work, Cassatt used one of her favorite subjects, a mother and child united physically in a relaxed and seemingly unposed manner, with a powerful and original composition. This work was probably inspired by Manet's *Boating* (Figure 50). Cassatt admired this painting and was instrumental in its purchase by her friends, Henry O. and Louisine Elder Havemeyer. However, Cassatt has transformed Manet's Impressionist work into a forceful post-Impressionist masterpiece.

While Manet positions his boat at a 45-degree angle to the picture surface, Cassatt aggressively foreshortens her boat so the viewer is thrust into the opposite end of the craft. Furthermore, there is no precedent in Manet's painting for the strong linear contours that subdivide the composition.

The Boating Party is carefully constructed to focus attention on the baby. Strong diagonal lines of the oar, the man's left arm, and the triangular sail all point to the child. The shadow bisecting the baby's face continues the bright white contour of the prow of the boat, as well as connecting the line formed by the upper edge of the sail, the rope, and the right edge of the prow. Cassatt's use of color is equally original. The juxtaposition of the bright yellow in the interior of the boat with the man's navy

FIGURE 49. MARY CASSATT. American, 1844–1926. *The Boating Party.* Canvas. 35 1/2 x 46 1/8'' (0.92 x 1.171). Date: 1893–1894. National Gallery of Art, Washington. Chester Dale Collection.

FIGURE 50. EDOUARD MANET, 1832–1883. *Boating*. Oil on canvas. 38 1/4 x 51 1/4'' (97.2 x 130.2 cm.). Signed (lower right): Manet. The Metropolitan Museum of Art, Bequest of Mrs. H. O. Havemeyer, 1929. The H. O. Havemeyer Collection. (29.100.115)

blue costume, all silhouetted against a highly saturated royal blue expanse of water, is both dramatic and effective in focusing the viewer's attention onto the canvas. By contrast, Manet's colors are much less intense, bleached by the sunlight in the more naturalistic manner of typical Impressionism.

Like her friend Degas, Cassatt was an ardent admirer of Japanese woodblock prints. The elevated viewpoint, high horizon line, and bright areas of relatively unmodeled color in *The Boating Party* are all elements derived from Japanese prints. For this painting, Cassatt utilized her recent experience in the creation of one of the murals for the Woman's Building at the Chicago World's Fair of 1893. The large scale, bright colors, and clearly defined, simplified contours of this painting are effective if the work is viewed from a distance. This mural, which has not survived, depicted an allegorical representation of *The Modern Woman*.

Cassatt also made an important contribution to the history of printmaking. In 1891, inspired by an exhibition of Japanese woodblock prints, she created a series of ten prints using an unprecedented technique. *The Fitting* (Figure 51) was created with a combination of etching and engraving techniques for the lines. Cassatt applied the beautiful and subtle earth-toned inks directly to the copper plate for each print. Each image is executed with the strictest economy of lines. This is particularly evident in the crouching figure of the seamstress. In *The Fitting,* the use of a mirror introduces a

FIGURE 51. MARY CAS-
SATT. *The Fitting Room*. 1891.
Drypoint, softground and aquatint. 14 3/4 x 10 1/8''. Museum
of Art, Carnegie Institute, Pittsburgh; Museum Purchase, 1919.

formal element of spatial complexity similar to the mirrored background in *The Loge*.
The image in the mirror is even more simplified than the "real" woman standing in
the room.

Mary Cassatt possessed both superb technical skills and great talent. Her dedication and devotion to the highest standards for her art helped her overcome the
"handicap" of being a woman. As an American in Paris, at a time when Paris was the
center of the art world, she absorbed the best innovations in her contemporary world
of painting. Cassatt developed an independent style based on precise draftsmanship,
refined color sensibility, and a gift for creative compositions.

PAULA MODERSOHN-BECKER
(1876–1907)

Before her premature death at the age of 31, Paula Modersohn-Becker developed an
innovative personal style based on a synthesis of French post-Impressionism and native German art forms. Her mature paintings, which include some recognized master-

pieces, reveal a talented and original artist whose works bear comparison with the best paintings of her European contemporaries in the post-Impressionist era.

Paula Becker was born in Dresden, Germany, into a cultured, upper-middle class family. She first became interested in becoming an artist when, at age 16, she was given art lessons as part of her finishing school education. Visiting wealthy relatives in London, she attended St. John's Wood School of Art, which prepared students for admission to the Royal Academy. Overcoming her parents' resistance, in 1896 she enrolled in Berlin in the art school for women run by the Verein der Kunstlerinnen, mentioned at the beginning of this chapter. Käthe Kollwitz had studied at this school nine years earlier.

After two years of this traditional instruction, Becker moved to the artists' colony located in Worpswede, a small village in northern Germany. The Worpswede artists, such as Fritz Mackensen and Otto Modersohn, used the local peasants and the bleak landscape as subjects and painted with a dark earth-toned, naturalistic palette. Becker studied with Mackensen and, at first, she adopted the realistic style of this painter.

On New Year's Eve, 1900, Becker left Worpswede for Paris. This was her first visit to the world's art capital. Over the next seven years, Becker spent long periods in Paris, where she acquired more art training and absorbed the latest developments in French avant-garde painting. Becker joined many other women artists who were studying art in Paris at the turn of the century. She worked at the Academie Colarossi where, for a small fee, an aspiring artist could paint or draw from the live model and receive some criticism from established masters. Becker also benefited from the recent opening of classes to women at the Ecole des Beaux-Arts.

Returning to Worpswede, Becker married the recently widowed Otto Modersohn in 1901. Even after marriage, Modersohn-Becker continued to make independent journeys to Paris. In 1903, 1905, and during a prolonged stay from February 1906 to April 1907, she abandoned the style of Worpswede naturalism for an avant-garde method that attained a greatly simplified monumentality.

Poorhouse Woman with a Glass Bowl (Figure 52) is both a portrait of a specific Worpswede woman, "Mother" Schroder, and a symbol of the stoical endurance of the peasants. Becker had drawn this old woman many times in the Worpswede poorhouse, an institution that sheltered destitute peasants during the winter.

Like the surrounding flowers that also decorate her skirt, this "Poorhouse Woman" survives each winter to work the soil with her enormous hands every spring. Flowers often symbolize the transience of life and the inevitability of death. In this work, however, the flowers may be seen as symbols of nature's cycle of perennial renewal. The shape of the glass bowl echoes Mother Schroder's ample form and flattened head. Both the woman and the bowl seem to grow directly from the earth.

Becker's use of simplified shapes, heavily outlined contours, and highly saturated colors all reveal the influence of Gauguin's Synthetism and Van Gogh's mature style. Like them, Becker's ability to create a nondescriptive image was based on careful study of natural phenomena. In 1903 she defined the goal for her art in the follow-

FIGURE 52. PAULA MODER-SOHN-BECKER. *Poorhouse Woman With a Glass Bowl.* 1906. Oil on canvas. 96 x 80.2 cm. Ludwig-Roselius Sammlung, Böttcherstrasse, Bremen.

ing way: "Generally through the most intimate observation to aspire to the greatest simplicity."[9] *Poorhouse Woman with a Glass Bowl* demonstrates Becker's ability to combine naturalistic observation and the stylistic innovations of the French avant-garde for the expression of a personal iconography.

Like Cassatt and Kollwitz, Becker also found the theme of the mother and child a continuously stimulating subject. *Kneeling Mother and Child* (Figure 53) is one of her most powerful and monumental versions of this theme. The figure is painted with thick, visible brushstrokes that assert the two-dimensional surface of the canvas and also firmly model the form. The enormous scale of the woman and her kneeling position on the isolation of the white cloth convey a sense of religious awe at woman's ability to create life and nourish an infant. The circle of fruits and the framing plants relate this modern "madonna" to the productivity of the earth itself. Her generalized features reinforce one's impression that this image is an icon dedicated to an Earth-Mother who symbolizes female fertility.

In this painting, Becker has created an image that is outside any historical framework, an impersonal archetype of fertility. As opposed to Cassatt's mothers and children, which are always portraits, or Kollwitz's mothers, who are forces for political change, Becker emphasizes the biology of creation. It is important to appreciate the different messages these images communicate. Women artists often approach the specifically female experience of maternity as well as every other subject in distinctive ways. Factors such as nationality, political views, and family background influ-

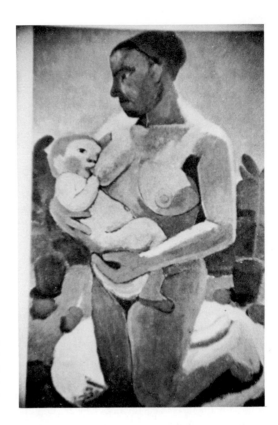

FIGURE 53. PAULA MOD-
ERSOHN-BECKER. *Kneeling
Mother and Child.* 1907. Oil on
canvas. 113 x 74 cm. Ludwig-
Roselius Sammlung, Böttcher-
strasse, Bremen.

ence the outlook and philosophy of an artist at least as much as, and perhaps more
than, the artist's sex. Becker's *Kneeling Mother and Child* is related more closely to
Gauguin's paintings of Tahitians than to the works of Cassatt or Kollwitz.

Otto Modersohn followed his wife to Paris in 1906. She became pregnant and
returned with him to Worpswede in 1907. It is possible that Becker was already pregnant when she painted *Kneeling Mother and Child.* She died three weeks after giving
birth to a daughter, tragically ending a career that had just reached maturity.
Nevertheless, she had lived long enough to create a group of paintings of great artistic
power and originality. As the first German artist to forge an original style that incorporated the innovations of French painting from the 1890s, her importance within the
European post-Impressionist avant-garde is firmly established.

chapter 10

Early Twentieth-Century Artists

Between 1900 and 1940 the pace of change in the art world, as in Western culture as a whole, accelerated dramatically compared with preceding centuries. A multiplicity of avant-garde movements altered the appearances and premises of painting more radically than in any period since the Renaissance. As women gained access to educational facilities, more and more women became professional artists in the twentieth century. Many elements of discrimination that had excluded women from participation in the fine arts in earlier epochs were no longer operative. Therefore, it is not surprising to find that women have participated not individually, but in groups, in almost every major avant-garde movement of the modern era.

Prior to World War I, a number of talented German artists focused their energies on the expression of a range of strong passions, using exaggerated, non-naturalistic formal means. Käthe Kollwitz was an expressionist who remained unaffiliated with any group movement. She created impressive works of art in the graphic media and in sculpture. Although nine years older than Modersohn-Becker, Kollwitz's expressionist style, which often reflected socialist political beliefs, is more directly related to early twentieth-century developments in German art than to late nineteenth-century post-Impressionism. For this reason, she is discussed in this chapter.

Between 1910 and 1920, a group of Russian artists, about half of whom were women, developed an abstract vocabulary based on geometric shapes for the creation of works of art that appear extremely modern even today. Under the initial impact of Cubism, the Russian avant-garde movements of Suprematism and Constructivism radically simplified the appearance of paintings. In collaboration with their male colleagues, Kasimir Malevich, Mikhail Larionov, and Vladimir Tatlin, women such as Natalia Goncharova, Liubov Popova, and Olga Rosanova created images that rejected virtually all elements of pictorial illusionism utilized by Western artists since the Renaissance. These Russian artists anticipated the extreme purity of Mondrian's neo-Plasticism, developed in Holland in the 1920s. Many of these women artists moved beyond the so-called fine arts to adapt their abstract styles for mass-produced objects, theater sets, costumes, and textile designs.

Sonia Terk-Delaunay was also a Russian artist famous for her personal abstract style. Because she spent her creative life in Paris, she is not considered a member of the Russian avant-garde, although her artistic concerns are closely related to those of her Russian compatriots. Prior to World War I, in collaboration with her husband, Robert Delaunay, she developed an abstract avant-garde style, ''Simultanism,'' which utilized brightly colored discs, creating effects of rhythmic movement and pulsating color. Delaunay's innovative style is a significant contribution to the history of twentieth-century modernism.

Surrealism was a major international style that affected developments in both the fine arts and literature in the 1920s and 1930s. Many artists in Europe and America were affected by the Surrealist premise that the artist should tap creative sources beneath the level of consciousness. Surrealist images attempt to illustrate a different reality from that which the conscious mind understands and the senses perceive. This ''sur-reality'' can originate in any number of sources, such as dreams, chance juxtapositions, or the artist's imagination. The Swiss Meret Oppenheim, the American Dorothea Tanning, and the Spaniard Ramedios Varo are among the numerous women artists whose works belong within the Surrealist movement. Many of the works of the ''Women of Surrealism'' relate specifically to female experiences and rank in quality with the best products of their male colleagues, such as Salvador Dali, Max Ernst, or René Magritte.

In America during the 1920s, Georgia O'Keeffe developed an original style of great simplification and monumentality. O'Keeffe's works do not often move into pure abstraction but retain an identification with nature. Unconnected with any specific movement, O'Keeffe is widely acknowledged as an exceptionally gifted artist who is among the very best American painters of the twentieth century.

By 1930 there were many women artists in America. A census of that year identifies 40 percent of all practicing American art professionals as women. Women were also prominent as administrators of federally funded arts projects during the Depression. These programs were notably free of sex bias; 40 percent of those receiving assistance were women. These statistics indicate that women artists were no longer interesting oddities or exceptions in a male dominated profession. From that time to the present, the percentage of art students and artists who are women has steadily grown.

Whether to consider photography an art and photographers artists, rather than technicians or craftsmen, has been the subject of debate since the invention of photography in the nineteenth century. Although most nineteenth-century authorities thought of photography more as a science or craft than as an art, the consensus today is that photography is indeed an art form. Photographs are collected, displayed in museums and galleries, and subjected to critical evaluation. Major photographers are the subjects of scholarly monographs. Photography has its own history, with recognized masters, which parallels the history of painting and sculpture. Therefore, while photographers are not generally discussed in standard art history texts, contemporary opinion justifies the inclusion of a select group of outstanding women photographers in this study.

Because photography was not regarded as an art in the late nineteenth and early twentieth centuries, the field was open to everyone without restrictions. Anyone who wanted to could make photographs, and no official schools controlled the dissemination of the technical knowledge necessary to practice photography. This made it possible for a number of women to achieve the first rank of excellence in the new medium. Women photographers, like women active in the fine arts, have created impressive images of a wide variety of subjects in many different photographic styles. As in the fine arts, women photographers were active participants in many avant-garde groups. The Englishwoman Julia Margaret Cameron was one of the most famous photographers of the late nineteenth century. Gertrude Käsebier, an American, was a "pictorial" photographer, active in the first decades of the twentieth century. Employing a softly focused style with simplified forms, she altered the conventions of portrait photography and narrative images. In contrast to Käsebier's style, Imogen Cunningham used a sharply focused, finely detailed technique. Working on the West Coast in the 1930s, Cunningham was a member of the Group f. 64, placing her in the avant-garde of her profession. Dorothea Lange and Margaret Bourke-White are noted photojournalists of the period. Both women began their careers documenting the poverty of America during the Depression. For almost thirty years, Bourke-White's photographs were reproduced in the popular magazines *Fortune* and *Life,* as well as in her own books. The widely disseminated photographs of these talented women shaped and altered the perceptions of contemporary Americans.

The women artists selected for discussion in this book overcame a variety of cultural and institutional obstacles to acquire the skills necessary for a career in the "fine arts," i.e., painting and sculpture. The vast majority of women did not have that opportunity. But like the photographers, women have found outlets for their visual creativity in ways which did not require specialized training. Sewing was one skill that all women have learned since antiquity. In the nineteenth and early twentieth centuries, many American women designed and fabricated quilts pieced from scraps of cloth. Many of these quilts are remarkably beautiful and original creations, worthy of consideration as works of art. These mostly anonymous women created visual images in cloth that demonstrate a high level of sophistication, anticipating some of the developments in twentieth-century abstract painting.

KÄTHE KOLLWITZ (1867–1945)

Käthe Kollwitz shares a common nationality and generation with Paula Modersohn-Becker. However, aside from the fact that both women created works of great force and originality often focused on women's primordial role as Mother, there are few similarities between them. While Becker retained a strong attachment to color and the medium of painting, Kollwitz, from the beginning of her career, concentrated on drawings and prints in black and white. Her self-imposed restriction to the graphic media stems from both personal inclination and political conviction. While still an art student, Kollwitz was fascinated by the demands of the printmaking process. She did not feel the need of color to express her powerful political messages. A print is less expensive than a painting because a number of original copies can be made from one source. Therefore, Kollwitz's graphics could be bought if not by the destitute workers, whom she depicted so sympathetically, then at least by the middle class people who shared her political beliefs.

Käthe Schmidt was born into an unusual family in the small Baltic seaport of Königsberg (now Kaliningrad). Her father was an ardent believer in socialism and an activist in the Social Democratic Worker's Party. Käthe absorbed these political beliefs, and throughout her lifetime her works express her sympathies for the oppressed poor and her strongly anti-capitalist convictions. Her family encouraged her artistic talents and gave her drawing lessons with a local artist. In 1885 she studied art in Berlin at the school for women established by the Verein der Kunstlerinnen. After a few years at home, in 1889 she entered the Verein's school in Munich where the cultural environment was more stimulating.

In 1884 she became engaged to Karl Kollwitz, who shared her family's political convictions. Fearful that marriage might interfere with her ambitions to become an artist, she postponed the wedding until 1891, when Karl had completed his medical studies and was a practicing doctor in a working-class neighborhood in Berlin. During the 1890s she bore two sons and worked on her first major graphic series, *The Revolt of the Weavers*, completed in 1897. The work was inspired by a play that told the true story of the 1844 armed rebellion of a group of destitute linen weavers in the German province of Silesia. This subject contains many recurrent themes that Kollwitz was to illustrate throughout the rest of her life: the misery of the impoverished working classes, the omnipresence of death, and a sympathy with armed revolt to improve inhuman conditions. *The Revolt of the Weavers* was greeted with great critical praise when it was displayed in 1898. The six prints that constitute this work established Kollwitz as one of Germany's leading graphic artists. Although she was nominated for a gold medal, the Kaiser denied her the award because of the radically leftist political content of the series.

Kollwitz's next major print cycle, *The Peasant War* (1902–8), was inspired by an uprising of German peasants in the sixteenth century. Kollwitz believed that women could be a force for political change, and she was attracted to this particular event because the leader of the revolt was a woman, Black Anna. *Outbreak* (Figure 54) depicts Black Anna inciting the men, who are armed with primitive weapons. In this extraordinarily powerful image, a peasant army races across the scene with an invincible force. Stylistically, Kollwitz retained enough descriptive details to characterize the individual features of the peasants, and there is an element of naturalism in the figure of Black Anna. The tension of the scene is intensified by presenting Black Anna with her back to the viewer. Kollwitz used her own body as a model for her great back. In this manner, emotion and energy are expressed

FIGURE 54. KÄTHE KOLLWITZ. *Outbreak*. 1903. Mixed technique. 20 x 23 1/4''. Courtesy of the Library of Congress.

through posture and gesture rather than mere facial expression. Technically, Kollwitz employed a mixture of etching techniques, aquatint, and soft ground to achieve the range of textures, shadings, and details of the finished work.

The experience of World War I was a great trauma for Kollwitz. In 1914 her son Peter was killed in Belgium. Kollwitz channeled her grief and fury into many prints in which she made statements against the futility of war and the destruction of young sons. The emotional content of *The Mothers* (Figure 55) must be understood in the context of the artist's intense revulsion toward the senseless killing of war. *The Mothers* is structured like a great sculptured bas-relief. Four women stand facing the viewer. The central figure and the one closest to us grasps her two children to her body in a protective embrace. Two other women hold their babies in their arms, and one figure uses her other arm to protect a small child. The fourth, the childless woman on the left, holds her hands to her face in a pathetic gesture of grief. The image is rendered in a drawing style that conveys energy and spontaneity. Compared with *Outbreak,* the style of *The Mothers* is greatly simplified, demonstrating the freedom of her mature draftsmanship.

Kollwitz's later works continue to explore the themes that had fascinated her

FIGURE 55. KÄTHE KOLLWITZ. *The Mothers.* 1919.
Lithograph. 17 3/4 x 23''. Philadelphia Museum of Art: Given
by an anonymous donor (46–79–1).

in her youth. Many images focus on the horrors of sudden death, the pains and
joys of motherhood, and the injustice of the economic exploitation and political
oppression of one class by another. Avoiding the abstraction and stylistic innovations
of many avant-garde artists, Kollwitz maintained a somewhat naturalistic style
throughout her career, although her works become more simplified and forms more
generalized in the 1920s and 1930s. Her talents were widely recognized during her
lifetime. In 1919 she became the first woman to be elected to the Prussian Academy
of the Arts. In 1928 she became director of graphic arts at this school. It was not
until the Nazis assumed power in Germany that, like so many other artists, she
experienced discrimination and was forced to resign from the Academy in 1933.

Kollwitz's compassion extended not only to the oppressed but also to her
fellow women artists who were not as famous as herself. She was elected president
of the Frauenkunstverband (Women's Art Union) in 1914. The main goal of this
group was "securing the right of women to teach and study in all public art
schools."[1] In 1926 she helped found GEDOK, (Society for Women Artists and
Friends of Art), a feminist organization that was "dedicated to showing, sponsoring,
and contributing to the work of women artists."[2]

Kollwitz continued working into her seventies. She witnessed the annihilation
of yet another generation of German youth in World War II. Her grandson Peter,
named after the son who had perished in World War I, also died in battle. The
works she left to posterity are loaded with the fullest possible range of human
emotions. Her images express her convictions as a woman, a mother, and a political
being. They are frequently painful and always emotionally stirring.

RUSSIAN WOMEN ARTISTS
OF THE AVANT-GARDE

A remarkable group of women artists were active participants in the pre-World War I avant-garde in Russia. Along with their male colleagues, they developed a totally abstract formal language for art, altering the basic vocabulary of painting. These artists, most of whom remained in Russia even after the Revolution of 1917, courageously explored the full range of possibilities of color, line, and shape in their art. Natalia Goncharova, Liubov Popova, and Olga Rosanova are among the most prominent Russian women in the avant-garde of this epoch. In the 1920s many of these artists designed textiles, stage sets, and other objects outside the realm of the ''fine arts.'' The concentration of women in this avant-garde movement is consistent with the international trend in the twentieth century in which women artists are more frequently active participants in radical groups.

In Russia, as in other countries of Europe, aristocratic women were often enthusiastic amateur painters. In 1842 the St. Petersburg Drawing School was opened to women. Later on there was a group of successful, if conservative, women artists active in the 1870s and 1880s, among whom Marie Bashkirtseff was perhaps the most famous. Such precedents established a base that at least partially explains the number of women artists in the pre- and post-Revolutionary Russian avant-garde.

The artists under consideration here unanimously rejected the Western Renaissance pictorial system. However, aside from their dedication to abstraction, their art shows great diversity and individuality. They all emerged from the same cultural matrix and share a solid position in the vanguard of the history of twentieth-century art.

Natalia Goncharova (1881–1962)

Natalia Goncharova is one of the most important and inventive figures of the Russian avant-garde. In 1898 she enrolled in the Moscow School of Painting, Sculpture and Architecture. She was one of the first artists to appreciate native Russian folk art forms and medieval icon paintings. In her works prior to 1912, she often combined the simplifications of these primitive art forms with the formal innovations and saturated colors of French Fauvism. Goncharova often depicted scenes from the urban environment, such as machines and electric lights, but she was also interested in the decorative potential of women's fashion accessories. In *Ostrich Feathers and Ribbons* (Figure 56), she arranges these female ornaments into an elegant, brightly colored composition. In this work three ribbons—navy blue, magenta, and rust—swirl and intertwine around the canvas. These linear forms seem to be moving because the eye must follow their sweeping patterns. Blue-black ostrich feathers provide another sort of curling form. She also uses white shapes that seem to be a fabric pierced with eyelet embroidery. The background of the upper half of the composition is brilliant orange dotted with red, and there is no

FIGURE 56. NATALIA GON-
CHAROVA. Russian, 1881–
1962. *Ostrich Feathers and Ribbons*. 1912. Oil on canvas. 35
1/8 x 27 1/2''. Courtesy Leonard
Hutton Galleries, New York.

recognizable three-dimensional space. It is not surprising that Goncharova was also
creating patterns for women's dresses and embroidery at this time. Her interest and
sensitivity to ornament evolved into a fascinating painting that works on a very
abstract level yet retains its connection with fashion accessories.

In 1912 Mikhail Larionov (1881–1964) began to use an aesthetic system
known as Rayonism. Related to Cubism and to Italian Futurism, Larionov's paintings
frequently depict the light rays that radiate from objects. Although some of Goncharova's works use a Rayonist style, she never pursued this system into the realm
of pure abstraction as Larionov did, and she never used it to the exclusion of other
styles. Goncharova maintained a separate and highly personal artistic identity despite
having lived with Larionov from 1900 on.

Goncharova's talents for the organization of decorative ensembles attracted
the attention of Serge Diaghilev, director of the Ballet Russe. Between 1914 and
1926, Goncharova designed the sets and costumes for several ballets for this company. She and Larionov joined the company in Paris in 1915. World War I prevented
their return to Russia, and after 1918 they settled permanently in Paris. Although
Goncharova's contribution to the history of art consists primarily in her pre-World
War I images, she continued to paint and produce book illustrations until the end
of her life.

Liubov Popova (1889–1924)

Another extremely important member of the Russian avant-garde was Liubov Popova. There is widespread scholarly agreement that Popova was an exceptionally gifted artist. She traveled to Paris in 1912 to study Cubism, and in the next years she painted in an abstract Cubo-Futurist style. Between 1918 and 1922, she developed a more personal style of radical simplification that makes her Cubist works look almost old-fashioned by comparison. "Her canvases illustrate the clearest and most consistent conception of Constructivism in painting to appear in the Soviet Union or anywhere else."[3] A typical example of this Constructivist style is *Painterly Architectonics* (Figure 57). This work consists of intersecting multicolored planes without any reference to objects in nature. Despite a certain amount of overlapping, it is impossible to say that these forms exist in a three-dimensional space. The traditional technique of modeling is employed nontraditionally because one cannot perceive these planes as rounded objects. Colors are also selected arbitrarily. This work is constructed with the most basic elements of painting, manipulated in a totally new way, overturning the Western tradition of painting since the Renaissance.

Popova and other women artists who painted in a Constructivist style became active in "production art," which included theater sets and costumes, industrial, graphic, and textile designs. As early as 1918, despite the political upheavals in Russia, the Visual Arts Section of the People's Commissariat for Enlightenment opened a special Subsection for Art-Industry, organized and directed by Olga Rosanova (1886–1918). The purpose of this group was to restructure the industrial

FIGURE 57. LYUBOV SERGEIEVNA POPOVA. *Architectonic Painting.* 1917. Oil on canvas. 31 1/2 x 38 5/8". Collection, The Museum of Modern Art, New York. Philip Johnson Fund.

design of the country. Rosanova encouraged many existing schools to join this organization.[4] She also devised a plan to reorganize the museums of industrial art in Moscow, which was eventually implemented. Many of her ideas were incorporated into the manifestos of Constructivism in the 1920s.

By 1924, Popova was working in the First State Textile Factory, designing new fabric patterns of great originality. She was very successful in transforming her refined and spare aesthetic sensibility, evident in her paintings, into textile designs. Using simple circles or arrangements of lines, Popova created patterns that seem to move back and forth in space. Such movement was more appropriate for fabrics than for paintings because the pattern had to enclose the three-dimensional body of the wearer.

Both the outstanding achievements of the Russian avant-garde as a whole and the extensive contribution of women artists to that achievement are appreciated today among scholars and critics. This movement changed the course of art history, anticipating many later developments in twentieth-century art. As we have seen, the women artists of this group were among the most radical and innovative artists in Russia, or indeed the world, at this time in history.

SONIA TERK-DELAUNAY (1885–1979)

Just before World War I, Sonia Delaunay created a painting system that employed brilliantly colored discs to create an effect of rhythmic movement. Her style, known as ''Simultanism,'' is an important and influential contribution to twentieth-century avant-garde painting. Like her countrywoman, Goncharova, Sonia Delaunay possessed a finely developed sensitivity to colors and their interrelationships.

Born in the Ukraine, at the age of five Sonia was adopted by her maternal uncle, Henry Terk, and raised in the wealthy, cultured environment of his home in St. Petersburg. Sonia Terk's artistic talents were encouraged, and from 1903 to 1905 she studied art in Germany. Her artistic training began in earnest when she arrived in Paris in 1905. Like Modersohn-Becker, who was also in Paris during these years, Terk absorbed the latest developments of French post-Impressionism and Fauvism.

In 1908 she had her first one-woman exhibition in the gallery of Wilhelm Uhde, but she did not exhibit her works in public again until 1953. The following year she married Uhde, but she divorced him in 1910 to marry the painter Robert Delaunay (1885–1941). Each of their talents complemented the other's, and their lives became a team effort that enhanced their individual gifts. Both Sonia and Robert Delaunay acknowledged the influence the other exerted on his or her art, especially between 1910 and 1914 when they both were formulating their definitive styles.

A major turning point in Sonia Delaunay's development was triggered by the creation of a quilt for her infant son, in 1911. Unlike the American quilt makers discussed later in this chapter, Delaunay was prepared to appreciate the possibilities of this abstract language for painting. The results of this breakthrough were soon visible in her works.

Electric Prisms (Figure 58) is one of her most important pre-World War I paintings. This large canvas (almost 8 feet square) was inspired by the electric lamps that had recently replaced gaslights on the Parisian boulevards. Using concentric circles divided into quadrants, the alternating and repeating colors create an optical effect of pulsating, brilliant light. These colored sections are arranged in a complex pattern of disks and are divided by straight lines and waving arc-like sections.

The exploration and depiction of ''colored rhythms'' or ''rhythms of color'' (both frequent titles of her works) was to be Delaunay's lifelong obsession. Her paintings, gouaches, and other two-dimensional works show a ceaseless inventiveness in the arrangement of colors to express movement and syncopation. Musical analogies seem unavoidable in the description of her pictorial language because she uses colored units like notes in a musical scale. Delaunay employs only the most basic elements of painting to construct her works. She defined her aesthetic system in the following way:

> The pure colors becoming planes and opposing each other by simultaneous contrasts create, for the first time, new constructed forms, not through chiaroscuro but through the depth of color itself.[5]

The term ''simultaneous contrasts'' refers to Chevreul's law, which states that when two complementary colors, such as red and green, are juxtaposed, their contrast is

FIGURE 58. SONIA DELAUNAY. *Electric Prisms*. 1914. Oil on canvas. 98 1/2 x 98 1/2''. Musee National d'Art Moderne, Centre Georges Pompidou, Paris.

intensified. Delaunay once explained her devotion to abstraction by stating: "Beauty refuses to submit to the constraint of meaning or description."[6]

Delaunay lost her personal income during the Russian Revolution, so after World War I, she turned increasingly to commercial, income-producing activities. She created several thousands of textile patterns as well as designs for fashions, book covers, tapestries, and many other objects. In the 1920s she designed "simultaneous" dresses and coats.

Clearly, the fact that Sonia Delaunay did not exhibit her paintings between 1908 and 1953 has affected the public's knowledge of her artistic achievement. However, since the 1950s her works are more widely known. Major retrospective exhibitions of her works were held in Paris in 1967 and in the United States in 1980. Sonia Delaunay has escaped the fate of many a woman artist married to another artist. Both Sonia and Robert Delaunay have received full recognition, individually and as a team, for their contributions to the history of art.

WOMEN OF SURREALISM[7]

There is an irony inherent in the Surrealist position on the nature of women, the "other" sex. André Breton, the leading theorist of the Surrealist movement, valued woman as a primal force that he viewed with respect and awe. He advanced definitions of woman as catalytic muse, visionary goddess, evil seductress, and most significantly, as *femme-enfant*, the woman-child whose naive and spontaneous innocence, uncorrupted by logic or reason, brings her into closer contact with the intuitive realm of the unconscious so crucial to Surrealism. Breton exalted woman as the primary source of artistic creativity, saying, "The time will come when the ideas of woman will be asserted at the expense of those of man."[8] However, Breton expected men to translate this intuitive woman's realm, viewed as closer to natural forces, into the culture as art. As flattering as his adulation of woman might seem, his theories relegated the "other" sex to the status of male-defined object, leaving little place for real women or women artists to develop independent identities. Thus, the women of Surrealism, as Gloria Orenstein has suggested in a landmark article, had to struggle against limitations placed on them by the very concepts of Surrealism itself.[9]

Yet Surrealism, as a movement that sought to explore altered states of consciousness, to penetrate the realm of dreams, and to make the imaginary real, includes a number of women who produced significant works. Meret Oppenheim, Remedios Varo, and Dorothea Tanning are among the leading women artists whose works fit within the Surrealist movement.

Meret Oppenheim (1913–   )

Raised in Switzerland and southern Germany, Meret Oppenheim went to Paris at the age of 18 to become an artist. She became the subject of some of Man Ray's most beautiful photographs, and in 1933 she was invited by Alberto Giacometti and Jean Arp to exhibit with the Surrealists. She continued to participate in their exhibitions until 1937 and again after World War II until 1960.

In the catalogue of Surrealist imagery, one piece stands out as the paradigm of the disturbing object: the fur-lined teacup of Meret Oppenheim. Although this work, alternately titled *Object* and *Fur Breakfast* (Figure 59), is frequently reproduced in standard texts, there is "a truly stunning absence of critical curiosity about Meret Oppenheim herself."[10]

Her fur-lined teacup remains a most potent example of the Surrealist goal to transform the familiar into the strange. Here, a mundane household object is rendered useless, while evoking the viewer's response to the sensation of drinking from wet fur. In another clever Surrealist object, Oppenheim trussed up a pair of women's high-heeled shoes like a holiday bird served on a silver platter, complete with paper frills. She also transformed a mirror by silk-screening onto the surface a face in the process of metamorphosis. She maintained a commitment to the ideas that formed the basis of Surrealism: "Artists, poets keep the passage to the unconscious open. . . . The unconscious is the only place from which help and advice can come to us."[11]

Many of the women artists of Surrealism have examined the specific creative

FIGURE 59. MERET OPPENHEIM. *Object.* 1936. Fur-covered cup, saucer, and spoon; cup, 4 3/8'' (10.9 cm.) diameter; saucer, 9 3/8'' (23.7 cm.) diameter; spoon, 8'' (20.2 cm.) long; overall height, 2 7/8'' (7.3 cm.). Collection, The Museum of Modern Art, New York. Purchase.

identity of Woman, not as muse to male creativity, but as an independent force. Although each has refined a complex, personal iconography, images recur in which woman is viewed as an alchemist or explorer, pursuing the mysteries of creation and creativity as a source of spiritual rebirth. This is particularly true in the work of Remedios Varo.

Remedios Varo (1913–1963)

Born in Spain, Remedios Varo became part of the Parisian Surrealist circle in the late 1930s. It was not until years later, however, from the distance of Mexico where she settled as a World War II exile, that she was able to develop a mature Surrealist vision and a distinctive painting style that evokes enthusiastic critical acclaim. Combining masterful rendering with a miniaturist's attention to detail, she created jewel-like compositions, small in size but monumental in scale. In a magical world of fantastic yet plausible events, she placed owl/artists, insect/geologists, crazed botanists, magical astronomers, and intrepid travelers who journey in fancifully invented vehicles or experiment in laboratories to find mystical sources and harmonies in the universe.[12]

In *Harmony* (Figure 60) an androgynous inventor is seated in a medieval-looking study filled with the tools of the alchemist. Taking objects from a treasure chest—geometric solids, jewels, plants, crystals, handwritten formulae—she places

FIGURE 60. REMEDIOS VARO. *Harmony.* Private collection.

them as notes onto a musical staff. From a chaos of possibilities, the order that is music is created. Like Pythagoras, she searches for the secret harmony that exists between nature and mathematics. In this work she is aided by phantom figures that emerge from behind peeling walls. These "collaborators" symbolize objective chance. In Varo's words, the Surrealist concept was "something which is outside of our world, or better said, beyond it. . . ."[13]

Much as Varo's work is an exploration of other realities, it is also a metaphor for the world in which she lived. As Varo's biographer, Janet Kaplan, has suggested, that virtually all the protagonists in Varo's paintings, whether male, female, or the ideal androgyne, bear a striking resemblance to the artist and should be understood as schematic self-portraits. Thus, it is Varo herself who is the alchemist or explorer. In creating these characters, she is defining her identity.

Dorothy Tanning (1910–   )

For Dorothea Tanning, too, personal identity can be seen as a central source of imagery. In her paintings women often appear placed in isolating and potentially menacing situations. One painting depicts young girls dressed in rags who seem haunted as they rip wallpaper into shreds along lonely corridors. In another work a woman, barefoot and half-clothed in a robe of dead branches, stands transfixed before a maze of doorways. She is accompanied by a fantastic creature with wings, tail, claws, and snout, who is her chimera or incubus.

Tanning's images speak to the condition of woman. This is most powerfully seen in *Maternity* (Figure 61). In this work a barefoot mother and child, dressed in identical sleeping cap and nightgown, stand between two open doorways in an otherwise barren landscape, tenderly hugging each other. Their only companion is a pet Pekinese dog whose face bears a strong resemblance to Tanning's own features as a child. Dark storm clouds fill the sky above a sulfurous yellow desert. In the background a menacing figure, half-organic, half-machine, looms through a distant doorway. The woman's gown is shredded over her abdomen as a distended belly and engorged breasts push through, suggesting the violent wrenching of birth and the strong biological link that inextricably binds mother to child. Maternity, that experience unique to women, is here expressed as tender but bitter, uniting but isolating, a door that opens to some experiences but closes off others.

Although born in the United States in 1910 and not associated with the Surrealists in France until the 1950s, Tanning felt that unknowingly, she had already become a Surrealist by the age of seven when, in the small town of Galesburg, Illinois, she composed messages to secret loves and sealed them in paper cubes. But it was only after seeing the "Fantastic Art, Dada and Surrealism" exhibition at New York's Museum of Modern Art in 1937 that she realized that her artistic personality could be understood as part of a larger movement. Upon meeting her future husband, the Surrealist artist Max Ernst, who had emigrated to the United States during World War II, the links between her art and Surrealism became more

FIGURE 61. DOROTHEA TAN-NING. *Maternity*. 1946. Oil on canvas. 44 x 57''. Private collection.

direct. Together they spent the 1940s in Sedona, Arizona, where Tanning produced many of her best known works. In the 1950s and 1960s while living in France, she combined her painting with scenery and costume design; during the 1970s she experimented with soft sculpture. She, too, remains true to Surrealist principles. "Me, I want to seduce by means of imperceptible passages from one reality to another."[14]

Oppenheim, Varo, and Tanning each developed an independent style through which she explored highly personal subject matter while remaining loyal to the basic tenets of Surrealism throughout her career. The research of the last decade, which has begun to recognize and evaluate the contributions of these artists, must be continued. Only then will Surrealism, a movement that exalted woman as the creative force, be understood and valued for the women creators within it.

GEORGIA O'KEEFFE (1887–   )

Georgia O'Keeffe is widely recognized as one of the best American painters of the twentieth century. A highly individual artist, she cannot be easily classified with any movement or school of painters. Although she is sometimes related to the Precisionists, such as Charles Sheeler, her largely organic abstractions and her painterly style separate her from the machine aesthetic of that group. O'Keeffe is truly an ''original''—an independent American who remained uninfluenced by the contemporary European abstract movements.

Born on a farm in Wisconsin, O'Keeffe acquired some academic training at the Art Institute of Chicago and then at the Art Students League in New York. In 1912 she was exposed to the teachings of Arthur Wesley Dow, one of the few art educators in America who rejected academic realism in favor of the simplifications and flat patterning of Oriental art.

Between 1912 and 1916, O'Keeffe spent winters teaching art in Amarillo, Texas. Inspired by the vast expanse of the plains and responsive to Dow's concepts, she began drawing abstract shapes that came from her internal visual imagination. In 1916 she sent a friend some of these drawings. Her friend took them to Alfred Stieglitz, the noted photographer, who ran a gallery in New York that showed avant-garde European and American works. The following year O'Keeffe had the first in a series of annual one-woman shows at Stieglitz's 291 Gallery. In 1924 she and Stieglitz were married, and they lived mostly in New York City until his death in 1946.

O'Keeffe's ability to distill abstract shapes from natural phenomena is never more apparent than in her famous paintings of flowers. In *Black Iris,* the flower is presented in a strictly frontal position, revealing its form to the viewer.[15] (This painting hangs behind Stieglitz in the Cunningham portrait (shown in Figure 64).) From the mysterious mauve darkness of its center, one's eye moves outward to the violet-gray veil-like shapes at the peak. The black-gray lower section forms a kind of base upon which the upper half of the flower is supported. O'Keeffe has explained the rationale for the creation of her flower paintings in the following way:

> Everyone has many associations with a flower. . . . Still—in a way—nobody sees a flower—really—it is so small—we haven't time—and to see takes time, like to have a friend takes time. If I could paint the flower exactly as I see it, no one would see what I see because I would paint it small like the flower is small.

> So I said to myself—I'll paint what I see—what the flower is to me but I'll paint it big and they will be surprised into taking time to look at it—I will make even busy New Yorkers take time to see what I see of flowers.

> Well I made you take time to look at what I saw and when you took time to really notice my flower you hung all your own associations with flowers on my flower and you write about my flower as if I think and see what you think and see of the flower—and I don't.[16]

The ''associations'' from which O'Keeffe separates herself refer to the connections often drawn between images such as *Black Iris* and women's sexual anatomy. It is a tribute to the power of O'Keeffe's works that they can evoke a broad range of associations that may vary from viewer to viewer. The relationship of this image to the female body is but one layer of metaphorical meaning that may be taken from it. Another interpretation might view it as fantasy architecture, an elaborate construction, or as a metaphor for a shelter, enclosure, or protection of a special being or sacred object. As Lloyd Goodrich has written, "The flower became a world in itself, a microcosm. Magnification was another kind of abstraction, of separating the object from ordinary reality, and endowing it with a life of its own."[17] The sheer formal power and brilliance of O'Keeffe's flower paintings secure their place among the most important American paintings of the twentieth century.

Beginning in 1929, O'Keeffe spent summers in New Mexico, where she felt a strong attraction to the stark beauties of the desert landscape. In addition to the geography of the desert, O'Keeffe repeatedly painted the bleached animal bones she found in the parched wilderness:

> When I found the beautiful white bones on the desert, I picked them up and took them home too. . . . I have used these things to say what is, to me, the wideness and wonder of the world as I live in it.[18]

Red Hills and Bones is an image that combines these animal bones with the actual landscape of the desert. In 1939 O'Keeffe explained her attraction for the desert badlands in the following way:

> The red hill is a piece of the badlands where even the grass is gone. Badlands roll away outside my door—hill after hill—red hills of apparently the same sort of earth that you mix with oil to make paint. All the earth colors of the painter's palette are out there in the many miles of badlands. The light Naples yellow through the ochres—orange and red and purple earth—even the soft earth greens. You have no associations with those hills—our waste land—I think our most beautiful country.[19]

Red Hills and Bones juxtaposes two bleached animal bones with rolling hills. Both hills and bones stretch across the full width of the canvas. The general shape of the two bones is echoed in the gently rounded mounds of the hills. Like the desert geography, the bones are both smooth and full of crevices. The openings between the vertebrae are related formally to the erosion creases of the distant hill.

In the statement just quoted, O'Keeffe mentions that the colors of the desert earth are the raw material for the painter's palette. The "red hills" of this painting are, in fact, painted in a range of saturated colors from violet through brick red to bright yellow. In this highly self-conscious painting, the realms of the natural world, the forms of animal skeletons and geography, are presented so the viewer becomes aware of their correspondence.

In 1949 after settling Stieglitz's estate, she moved permanently to the remote town of Abiquiu, New Mexico. Now in her nineties, she lives there still. O'Keeffe's art—spare, clear, and powerful—forces us to see that portion of nature she explored in a new and more profound way.

WOMEN PHOTOGRAPHERS
BEFORE WORLD WAR II

As noted in the introduction to this chapter, because photography was not considered an art, women experienced no overt institutional discrimination in acquiring the skills necessary to become photographers. That accounts for the number of outstanding women photographers whose achievements are widely recognized in the history of photography. Women photographers, like women painters, worked in a wide variety of styles and with an equally broad range of subjects.

Julia Margaret Cameron (1815–1879)

One important woman photographer from the nineteenth century to achieve success and recognition from her works is Julia Margaret Cameron. Julia Pattle was born in Calcutta, India. Her father was a wealthy merchant in the East India Company. After being educated in France and England, Julia returned to Calcutta at age 19. A few years later, she met Charles Hay Cameron, an upper-class Englishman, and they were married in 1838. Cameron, twenty years older than Julia, was an eminent jurist who codified the Indian statutes. In 1848, the couple returned to England, and in 1860, they settled on the fairly isolated Isle of Wight. Julia Cameron took up photography at the age of 48 as a diversion because her six children were grown and her husband was frequently away on business. Although she had no formal training and her knowledge of photography came from popular manuals and trial and error, she attacked the new medium with characteristic energy and enthusiasm.

In her time, Cameron was best known for her romantic, unfocused photographs. She often recorded sentimental allegories, influenced by the subjects of pre-Raphaelite paintings. Today, however, her portraits are considered her best works. The Camerons were part of Britain's social and intellectual elite, friendly with many of the most notable Englishmen of the era, who often visited the family on the Isle of Wight. Among her illustrious sitters were the painters George Watts and William Holman Hunt, the poets Alfred, Lord Tennyson and Robert Browning, and the scientist, Charles Darwin. She also used family members as sitters. The photograph of her niece, Julia Jackson, taken in April 1867 (Figure 62) is a typical example of her portrait style. Julia Jackson, wife of Herbert Duckworth, was the mother of Virginia Woolf, one of the most important writers of the twentieth century. The eminent art critic Roger Fry has termed this portrait ''a splendid success,'' noting further that ''the transitions of tone in the cheek and the delicate suggestions of reflected light, no less than the beautiful 'drawing' of the profile, are perfectly satisfying.''[20] In a tribute to Cameron written in 1926, Fry asserts the validity of considering photography an art form and refers to her as the ''most distinguished'' artist-photographer who ever lived.

FIGURE 62. JULIA MARGA-
RET CAMERON. *Portrait of
Mrs. Herbert Duckworth*. 1867.
Silver print. 12 1/2 x 10 1/4''.
Collection B. and N. Newhall,
The George Eastman House,
Rochester, New York.

Gertrude Käsebier (1852–1934)

Gertrude Käsebier, one of America's most noted photographers around the
beginning of the twentieth century, is famous as both a portrait photographer and
a pictorialist. Like Cameron, Käsebier used posed situations to express sentimental
scenarios, and also like Cameron, Käsebier became a photographer rather late in
life, and in a similarly unplanned encounter with the medium. Gertrude Stanton
was born in the frontier settlement of Fort Des Moines, Iowa. The Colorado gold
rush drew her father to Eureka Gulch, where the family lived from 1860 to 1864.
After her father's death, when Gertrude was 12 years old, the family settled in New
York City. Gertrude received a proper middle-class education and, in 1874, married
a German, Eduard Käsebier, a shellac importer. She broke out of the typical pattern
of Victorian wife and mother (the couple had three children) when she enrolled in
Pratt Institute in 1889 to study portrait painting. Käsebier's interest in photography
began in a casual, amateur manner while making photographs of her family. During
a summer spent studying painting in France, she made her first indoor portrait and

soon thereafter decided that portrait photography, not painting, was her true vocation. From 1897 on, Käsebier operated a successful and fashionable portrait photography studio in New York City. Utilizing her knowledge of painting, she elevated the portrait photograph to the status of an art form. William Homer believes that this is her most important contribution to the history of photography. "In her commercial portraits, she was the first to break away from the stilted, artificial, and overly detailed images that were so common in the professional studios of her day in favor of effects that were simple, dignified, and artistic."[21] Her style was widely praised and imitated by other commercial portrait photographers.

Around 1900, Käsebier began to make photographs that were not simple portraits, for they used sitters as actors in situations that conveyed symbolic themes. In this manner she entered the ranks of the "pictorial photographers." Stylistically, she avoided specific details and sharp focus, striving for a moody, generalized image also favored by contemporary painters active in Europe, such as James A. McNeill Whistler and Eugène Carrière.

Käsebier often used the subject of maternity as her theme—sometimes in an idealized manner, at other times in an ironical one. Her most famous photograph, *Blessed Art Thou Among Women* (Figure 63), is both a portrait of her friend Frances Lee and her daughter and a symbol of the joys of maternity. The title, which alludes to the biblical Annunciation carried to Mary by the Angel, is lettered on the picture frame in the background. The white tones of the door frame are elegantly echoed in the white gown of the mother and contrasted with the dark upright form of the little girl. Simple, yet effective, the image expresses the protective, nurturing aspect of motherhood and its fulfillment as a religious duty. The following year Käsebier photographed Frances Lee again in *The Heritage of Motherhood* (ca. 1900). This time, the sitter is positioned alone on a cliff, hands clasped together. This photograph expresses the theme of a mother's fortitude and endurance when she is left alone after her children have grown.

Between 1902 and 1913, Käsebier was a member of the Photo-Secession, an avant-garde group founded by Alfred Stieglitz. The Photo-Secession was an influential group that promoted the acceptance of photography as an art form. To disseminate these views, Stieglitz published the journal *Camera Work*. The first issue, in 1902, was dedicated to Käsebier's photographs, thus securely establishing her reputation as one of the foremost photographers of her time. Käsebier was also one of the most technically expert and prolific in the field. She experimented with a very wide variety of printing processes and created the extraordinary number of 100,000 negatives during the course of her career.

Imogen Cunningham (1883–1976)

Along with Edward Weston and Ansel Adams, Imogen Cunningham is known for her sharply focused images of natural phenomena. Reacting against the style of "pictorial photography" favored by Stieglitz and Käsebier, these San Francisco

FIGURE 63. GERTRUDE KASE-
BIER. *Blessed Art thou Among
Women.* c. 1900. Platinum print
on Japanese tissue. 9 3/8 x 5 1/2''.
Collection, The Museum of Mod-
ern Art, New York. Gift of Mrs.
Hermine M. Turner.

photographers formed a rather unstructured organization known as the Group f. 64.
An f. 64 setting on a camera is a very small lens opening and it gives a sharply
focused, finely detailed image along with a greater depth of field. Through the
1930s the Group f. 64 was the most influential photography society in the country.
Among Cunningham's most famous photos are very close-up studies of flowers
and plants with strong light-dark contrast. This type of subject, as we have seen,
was also favored by O'Keeffe. Cunningham's portrait of Stieglitz (Figure 64) is
typical of her style in its strong light and dark contrasts, sharp textural definition,
and psychological insight. Behind Stieglitz hangs O'Keeffe's *Black Iris,* discussed
earlier. Cunningham's portrait is a tribute to this couple—the master photographer
and the great painter.

Dorothea Lange (1895–1965)

Born of German immigrant stock in Hoboken, New Jersey, Dorothea Lange
had decided to become a photographer by the time she was seventeen years old.

FIGURE 64. IMOGEN CUN-
NINGHAM. *Alfred Stieglitz,
Photographer, 1934.* © 1970 The
Imogen Cunningham Trust.

While attending courses to become an elementary school teacher, she worked in
several photographers' studios in New York learning her craft. Leaving home with
a girl friend, Lange settled in San Francisco in 1918, where she established herself,
like Käsebier, as a professional portrait photographer.

Lange's contribution to the history of photography dates from the 1930s,
when she was hired by the Farm Security Administration both to document the
plight of the migrant workers and to arouse sympathy for federal relief programs
to aid them. *Migrant Mother* (Figure 65) is the most famous photograph from this
program. The circumstances surrounding the encounter with the subject of *Migrant
Mother* have an almost eerie quality of intuitive recognition. Lange said, "I drove
into that wet and soggy camp and parked my car like a homing pigeon."[22] This
woman was only 32 years old. She and her children had been surviving on frozen
vegetables gleaned from the fields and birds caught by the children. There was no
more work since the pea crop had frozen. They could not move on because the car
tires had just been sold to buy food. We do not really need to know this background
saga of desperation. The anguish on this woman's face, her children who hide their
faces from the photographer—these are immediately recognizable symbols of extreme poverty and stoical endurance. In fact, the image conveys this information
so directly and eloquently that it has become one of the most memorable pictures
of the last 50 years.

FIGURE   65. DOROTHEA
LANGE. *Migrant Mother, Nipo-
mo, California.* 1936. Gelatin-
silver print. 12 1/2 x 9 7/8''. Collection, The Museum of Modern
Art, New York. Purchase.

Margaret Bourke-White (1904–1971)

Like Dorothea Lange, Margaret Bourke-White was a documentary photographer, and she is remembered as one of the most famous and prolific American
photojournalists. Born in New York, she was an active amateur photographer by
her freshman year at the University of Michigan, in 1921. Her professional career
began in Cleveland in 1927, following the collapse of a two-year marriage. In 1929
she was hired as a staff photographer for a new magazine, *Fortune,* published by
Henry Luce. When Luce founded the magazine *Life* in 1936, Bourke-White was
hired as one of its four original staff photographers. She continued to work for the
immensely popular *Life* until 1956, when the debilitating effects of Parkinson's
disease forced her into retirement.

Bourke-White was an aggressive, fearless, documentary photographer. She
traveled the globe in pursuit of images to inform the American people of the major
world events of the epoch. Her courage and determination to get the right photo
are legendary. She understood her works as historical documents and, in fact, her
images shaped the consciousness of millions.

Bourke-White traveled through the Dustbowl of America's Midwest in the
1930s, recording the daily lives and the effects of poverty on the people of small-town
America. Like the works of Lange, Bourke-White's images forced the readers of

Life magazine to empathize with the plight of the unfortunate and destitute people captured in her photographs. *At the Time of the Louisville Flood, 1937* (Figure 66), one of her most famous photographs, depicts homeless refugees lining up for emergency supplies. The juxtaposition of these impoverished blacks and the billboard behind them proclaiming the prosperity of the "typical" American family is ironic social commentary.

Bourke-White was a courageous war photojournalist. At the end of World War II she arrived with General Patton to record the liberation of Buchenwald, one of the Nazi concentration camps. Her photograph of the emaciated and expressionless survivors, *The Living Dead of Buchenwald, Apirl 1945* (Figure 67) became an unforgettable image of the Holocaust. Bourke-White recorded her reactions to this experience in her book, *Dear Fatherland, Rest Quietly:*

> I kept telling myself that I would believe the indescribably horrible sight in the courtyard before me only when I had a chance to look at my own photographs. Using the camera was almost a relief; it interposed a slight barrier between myself and the white horror in front of me . . . it made me ashamed to be a member of the human race.[23]

According to Beaumont Newhall, author of the definitive *History of Photography,* one personality trait that unites these women photographers is "drive"—a combination of determination, persistence, and energy. Despite stylistic differences,

FIGURE 66. MARGARET BOURKE-WHITE. *Louisville Flood Victims, 1937.* Life Magazine © 1937 Time Inc.

FIGURE 67. MARGARET BOURKE-WHITE. *The Living Dead of Buchenwald, April 1945.* Life Magazine © 1945 Time Inc.

each photographer possessed great force of personality that accounts, in part, for her success in this medium.

AMERICAN PIECED QUILTS

Since time immemorial, sewing has been an occupation associated with women. But sewn objects, except for the works of medieval embroidery discussed in Chapter 2, usually do not have a place in the history of art. However, during the nineteenth century in America, the design and fabrication of quilts, pieced together from leftover bits of cloth, produced many works of extreme complexity and sophistication. One such example is the anonymous quilt created with the pattern known as "Log Cabin, Barn Raising" (Figure 68).

Unlike many Victorian designs for objects of daily use, quilts are made with geometric shapes because straight edges are the easiest to sew together. From the scraps of fabric left over from clothing, square units of uniform size were stitched together. These individual squares were then arranged to form the overall design of the quilt. Some quilts used identical blocks creating a repeating pattern, while others, such as the example illustrated here, used differing blocks. The cutting of each piece to be fitted into the patchwork quilt had to be extremely accurate so the blocks would fit together precisely.

This "Log Cabin, Barn Raising" quilt employs a broad sampling of late nineteenth-century cotton calico fabrics. Most are printed in small, closely spaced

FIGURE 68. *Log Cabin Barn Raising Quilt.* Dechert Price & Rhoads, Philadelphia, Pa.

patterns popular at this time. The lighter tones are mostly from fabrics used for men's shirts. After cutting, the bits of fabric were sewn into the basic unit, known as the ''Log Cabin.'' Each individual square or block contains strips of fabric usually cut into right angles or pieced into this shape from smaller scraps. The sections of fabric fit together into a telescoping pattern until there is a small square in the center. Each of the units is divided diagonally into a dark and a light-toned triangle. The individual blocks are then assembled so that the light-dark modulations create an overall pattern of diamonds called the ''Barn Raising.'' The term is derived from the resemblance of the pattern to the sections of a barn wall laid flat on the ground before it is built. Thus, the main design elements of this quilt are abstracted from vernacular architecture. One may even see the corner blocks as the ''cornerstones'' of the quilt.

Despite these references to architecture, the quilt functions visually as a two-dimensional ''painting.'' The patterns of the fabric emphasize the flat surface of the quilt. The light-dark transitions are carefully modulated to avoid a forceful effect of movement forward and backward in space. The color scheme is dominated by cool blues, greens, and earth tones. The border is a dark midnight blue. The combinations of different fabrics indicate a refined sensitivity to color.

Once the top layer of the quilt was stitched together, it was joined to a solid backing and a filler of cotton or wool was sandwiched in-between. The three layers were joined by the quilting technique itself. This final quilting was often accomplished at a social gathering known as a "quilting bee." Quilting bees were a valid pretext for a party, breaking the often oppressive isolation of rural life.

Quilts served a very practical function at home. They covered beds and kept the sleeper warm. However, quilts were also a conspicuous demonstration of the skills of their creators. Pride, care, and effort were lavished on them. Long after the invention of the sewing machine, quilts were sewn by hand. Women made quilts as part of their dowry and mothers made a quilt for each child. The creation of quilts was intertwined with the cycle of women's lives.

From the perspective of the twentieth century, we are prepared to appreciate these quilts with their geometric designs as works of art in their own right. The anonymous creator of this quilt did not possess the specialized training available to the painters discussed in this chapter. She used a readily available and economical technique, i.e., sewing bits of leftover fabric, as the means to create a beautiful, abstract image that expresses an individual visual sensibility.

chapter 11

Artists of the Post-World War II Era

Women artists have been increasingly influential and active as equal participants in the full range of developments in painting and sculpture since World War II. A cursory overview of works by women artists during this most recent epoch indicates that sex alone is not a strong enough factor to determine any particular predisposition toward a specific style of art. The large numbers of women artists, of whom only a handful of the most outstanding have been selected for discussion in this chapter, have worked in a wide variety of styles in the most diverse media imaginable. In the absence of institutional barriers and with the increased equality of women in all phases of the postwar culture, women artists have demonstrated in the past few decades that they are capable of originality and can achieve the highest levels of creativity in the visual arts.

Unlike earlier centuries, when prominent sculptors like Hosmer were rare indeed, there have been many important and influential women sculptors in the twentieth century. Germaine Richier and Barbara Hepworth are among the major sculptors of recent decades. Richier, a Frenchwoman and contemporary of Giacometti, used the traditional method of bronze casting to create a series of figurative works that reveal a personal style and iconography. Her major pieces date from the 1950s and combine elements of Surrealism and Expressionism in a synthesis of originality and force.

Hepworth is generally acknowledged as one of England's most important sculptors. A contemporary and colleague of Henry Moore, Hepworth's art also employs an abstract, biomorphic vocabulary. Beginning in the late 1920s and continuing into the 1970s, her art continuously explores the archetypal correspondences between humanity and the natural world. Unlike Richier, who modeled her works and then cast them into bronze, Hepworth developed her style through the process of direct carving.

Louise Nevelson's contribution to the history of modern art derives primarily from the invention of a new method to create large-scale, monumental sculpture. In the late 1950s, she gathered together small pieces of wood, arranged them into compositions within boxes, then piled these units together to form large environmental structures. Employing this assemblage technique on a much larger scale and in a manner different from any previous artist, Nevelson opened up a whole new range of possibilities for the creation of sculpture. Her originality is undisputed and she is generally considered one of the most important American sculptors of the post-World War II era.

In painting, Abstract Expressionism was the first major American painting movement to develop independently of European influences after World War II. Arshile Gorky, Jackson Pollock, Willem de Kooning, and Franz Kline are the major figures in the first generation of Abstract Expressionists. These artists relied primarily on the gestural application of pigments to convey emotional content. Helen Frankenthaler is recognized as one of the major figures in the second generation of Abstract Expressionists for her invention of the ''soak-stain'' technique in 1952. Instead of using pigments, which retain the imprint of the brush, or the viscous textures of Pollock's ''drip'' technique, Frankenthaler thinned the paint so it soaked into the canvas, creating a very luminous and lyrical effect. By the late 1950s, a number of artists in the second generation of Abstract Expressionists, such as Morris Louis, Kenneth Noland, and Paul Jenkins, were exploring the possibilities of this new method of paint application, pioneered by Frankenthaler.

While Frankenthaler's method was one form of response to the dominance of the painterly gesture of Abstract Expressionism, by the late 1950s another group of painters known as Minimalists were exploring other methods to create works of art. Minimalism, as a movement, asserted the importance of holistic systems, hard edges, immaculate surfaces, and geometric forms. Elsworth Kelly, Ad Reinhart, Barnett Newman, and Agnes Martin were among the first artists to use simplified systemic and symmetrical formats for their paintings. Martin's most characteristic works employ a grid format, pencilled onto a pale and uniformly colored surface. Through the grid, Martin retained an intensified, conceptual control over the creation of the work of art. The use of a grid was as different as possible from the random and seemingly spontaneous methods of Abstract Expressionism.

Minimalism developed contemporaneously with both Pop Art and Op Art in the early 1960s. All these painting movements reacted against the ''action painting'' of Abstract Expressionism. Artists used serial imagery, immaculate surfaces, and geometric shapes to order the picture surface. Op Art, the nickname for ''Optical Art,'' examined the actual processes of visual perception. Bridget Riley was in the forefront of this movement, creating images in black and white in the early 1960s that epitomized this concentration on the physiology of vision.

In the Pop Art movement of the 1960s, no women played roles comparable to artists such as Robert Rauschenberg, Jasper Johns, or Roy Lichtenstein. However, Afro-American artists Betye Saar and Faith Ringgold, among others, recognized in the 1960s and 1970s the potency of combining pre-coded material from popular culture into works with militant messages of black liberation. Both artists reacted against the distinctions between "fine arts" and "crafts," and both developed innovative styles for their works.

The avant garde sculptures of Eva Hesse and Louise Bourgeois share common elements. Their works are often small scale and non-geometric in form, and they frequently use unusual materials, such as string, wire, or rubber latex. Their images most frequently make some reference to organic forms or human sexuality. In place of the seriousness and architectural pretensions of minimal sculpture, both artists invented post-minimal styles based on highly personal symbol systems with clear references to the human body.

Audrey Flack, like Richard Estes and Don Eddy, is one of the major figures in the 1970s movement known as Photo Realism, Super Realism, or New Realism. These artists use color slides as sources for paintings created with an air brush and thus related in appearance to large-scale advertisements, such as images on billboards. Rather than selecting a given scene from her environment, like other Photo Realists, Flack's paintings are still lifes that employ a highly personal content.

The artists discussed in this chapter are not the only women creators to make important contributions to the history of modern art. They have been selected for detailed discussion because each figure is an outstanding representative of a major avant-garde movement in contemporary art history. The achievements of these few artists do not represent the total contribution of women to the visual arts. There are many other women artists working today whose works are also worthy of attention and recognition.

GERMAINE RICHIER (1904–1959)

The sculpture of Germaine Richier combines elements of Expressionism with the dream world of Surrealism. Using the traditional technique of bronze casting, Richier evolved a personal sculptural style that deals with themes of growth and decay, terror and violence. Richier makes archetypal images—symbolic forms through which she explores the mythic dimensions of human experience.

Richier was born on a farm near Arles in the south of France. Raised in close contact with nature, her childhood fascination with the insect life of the region reappears in her art. In works such as *The Preying Mantis* or *The Batman*, she transforms a human figure into something primeval and animal.

Richier's interest in making sculpture can be traced back to her early youth. She told an interviewer: "I had always wanted to do sculpture, without painting as a transitional state. I didn't draw. What excited me was building."[1] Following three years of study at the Montpellier Ecole des Beaux-Arts, Richier arrived in Paris in 1925. There, she entered the studio of the noted sculptor Antoine Bourdelle. Although she remained with Bourdelle for four years, her mature sculptural style is more closely related to the Surrealist distortions of Giacometti, whom she met in Bourdelle's studio, than to the more classical vision of Bourdelle himself.

Richier's sculpture began to receive recognition in the 1930s. During World War II, she and her Swiss husband lived in neutral Zurich. Although she made sculpture during the war years, her most famous works date from the early 1950s. In *Water* (Figure 69), one can see the characteristic pitted surfaces of her images. Her figures often appear to be eroded over time, like ancient artifacts. In this work, the spindly arms, legs, and thin base are contrasted to the massive volume of the body of a woman. This is a typical characteristic of Richier's sculpture: "I like thin legs supporting heavy masses . . . [other sculptors] made thick legs when sculpture had a respect for the canon. This, I do not care to maintain."[2]

At the neck, the two handles refer to the form of a Greek amphora, or vase. The concept of the female as a container or vessel is very ancient. One of the attributes of the primordial female deity, the "Great Goddess," was a divine water jug. The Great Goddess "is mistress of the upper waters, the rain; and the lower waters, the brooks and streams that spring from the womb of the earth."[3] The fertility of woman was associated with the waters of life that, like amniotic fluid and rain, were believed to be magically connected with the giving of life. The potential of the female body to contain a child related woman metaphorically to the concept of a vessel. Possibly the ancient activity of women who made containers, especially pottery, served to confirm this association. Richier transforms this mythological concept, also used by her contemporaries Henri Matisse and Pablo Picasso, into an impressive sculptural statement.

FIGURE 69. GERMAINE RICH-IER. *Water*. 1953–54. The Tate Gallery, London.

While *Water* expresses the life-giving potential of the female body, many of Richier's works evoke a shudder of imminent mortality. Both the expressive elongations and the corroded or pitted surfaces she uses so frequently serve to convey a sense of material decay. This dematerialization of the flesh can be rather frightening. Reflecting the anguish of two world wars, Richier did not avoid the darker emotions of the human condition. Her figures were always set in isolation, not placed into social interaction. Thus, they convey the existential loneliness of the modern era. "We southerners . . . look cheerful, but beneath the surface a drama is buried. Arles is a tragic town."[4] Although Richier's art is not widely known, she created an original group of works that convey powerful emotional content.

BARBARA HEPWORTH (1903–1975)

Barbara Hepworth is one of England's most internationally celebrated sculptors. Like Henry Moore, with whom she is frequently compared, Hepworth employs a personal vocabulary of organically abstracted shapes and forms to create her works. Primarily through the technique of direct carving, Hepworth's art explores the fascinatingly complex relationship between man and nature.

Hepworth's earliest memories are of the Yorkshire landscape in which she was born. Her father was a surveyor, and as a child she accompanied him on his trips. In her autobiography she states:

All my early memories are of forms and shapes and textures. Moving through and over the West Riding landscape with my father in his car, the hills were sculptures; the roads defined the form. Above all, there was the sensation of moving physically over the contours of fulnesses and concavities, through hollows and over peaks—feeling, touching, seeing, through mind and hand and eye. This sensation has never left me. I, the sculptor, am the landscape. I am the form and I am the hollow, the thrust and the contour.[5]

At age sixteen she won a scholarship to the Leeds School of Art, where she met Henry Moore. The following year Hepworth and Moore enrolled in the Royal College of Art in London. In 1924 they were both awarded travel fellowships. Hepworth went to Italy, where she learned the technique of marble carving.

Although Hepworth married a sculptor, John Skeaping, in 1925, the most important artistic and personal alliance of her life was with the painter Ben Nicolson. They were married in 1931 and shortly thereafter traveled to Paris to visit the studios of Constantin Brancusi and Jean Arp. The works of these sculptors encouraged Hepworth to move toward an increasing simplification and to use biomorphic, but totally abstract, shapes in her art. After the birth of triplets in 1934, Hepworth eliminated all references to natural forms in her work and employed a totally abstract, geometric vocabulary. "I was absorbed in the relationships in space, in size and texture and weight, as well as in the tensions between the forms."[6]

Like Moore, Hepworth was fascinated with the action of piercing the solid mass to reveal the negative shape. As early as 1931, she explored the potential of the concavity and the void. Beginning in 1947, Hepworth developed a renewed interest in the human figure that had not appeared in her art since the 1920s. Both these concerns are clearly expressed in *Two Figures* (Figure 70). The solid forms of the wood have been hollowed out so that large portions of their core sections are revealed. This carving process is further emphasized by the concavities, which are painted white. Each form is also pierced by two holes, accentuating the contrast between solid and void.

These "figures," upright like humans, are related but not identical. The shapes of their exterior contours and interior hollows are quite different. One has the urge to identify them as "male" and "female," but it is impossible to determine which is which.

Prior to 1956, Hepworth used only the technique of direct carving to make her sculpture. In that year she began modeling works in plaster and then casting the forms into bronze. The most famous and important work Hepworth executed in bronze is the great monolith, *Single Form* (Figure 71), dedicated as a memorial to Dag Hammarskjöld, former director of the United Nations. The *Single Form* is a soaring shape, 21 feet tall, broader at the top than at the base. It is constructed from six large slabs of bronze. The lines that mark the divisions between the pieces subdivide its planar surface. A large hole is the most significant accent of the work, relating this sculpture to Hepworth's other forms, which frequently incorporate voids. The *Single Form* is a proud, noble shape recalling the massive uprights of Stonehenge. Its primitive simplicity increases its impression of monumentality.

FIGURE 70. BARBARA HEPWORTH. English, 1903–1975. *Two Figures*. 1947–48. Elmwood with white paint. H.: 38 x 17". University Gallery, University of Minnesota, Minneapolis. John Rood Sculpture Collection.

FIGURE 71. BARBARA HEP-
WORTH. *Single Form.* 1964.
Bronze, mounted on granite base.
H.: 21'. Gift of Jacob Blaustein
in memory of Dag Hammar-
skjold. Courtesy United Nations,
New York.

Hepworth's career punctures many stereotypical misconceptions about women
artists, particularly women sculptors. For much of her career, she created her works
through carving. Clearly, male physical strength is no prerequisite for the sculptor's
craft. In the *Single Form*, she proved that she could sustain her vision on a monumental scale. And although married to two artists, she managed to maintain her
professional identity and individuality. Today, Hepworth's reputation is secure. She
is widely recognized as an important innovator in the realm of organically abstract
sculpture.

In 1968 the importance of Hepworth's oeuvre was recognized with a major
retrospective exhibition at the Tate Gallery in London. Her works are in most major
museum collections and the bibliography on her art is extensive. She worked continuously at making sculpture until her death in a studio fire in 1975.

HELEN FRANKENTHALER (1928–   )

Helen Frankenthaler is one of the major figures in the second generation of Abstract
Expressionists. Her prominent position in the history of modern painting is secure

because she invented a highly influential method of paint application known as the "soak-stain" technique. While O'Keeffe paints identifiable objects to reveal their abstract qualities, Frankenthaler uses abstract shapes to evoke the forms of the natural world.

Frankenthaler was born into a distinguished upper middle-class family. Her father was a Justice of the New York State Supreme Court. Frankenthaler received an elite, private school education in New York City. According to her own recollection, by age fifteen or sixteen she had decided to become an artist. She attended Bennington College where she painted in a Cubist style. Then, upon graduation in 1949, she returned to New York where the influential critic Clement Greenberg introduced her to the leading male artists of Abstract Expressionism.

Frankenthaler's historically most significant painting is *Mountains and Sea* (Figure 72), created in 1952. The canvas stretches almost 10 feet across. Inspired by Pollock's murals, which he placed on the floor and worked from all four sides, Frankenthaler used the same method. Edges were defined after the canvas was painted. However, Pollock's drip technique retained the thick texture of the paint, whereas Frankenthaler found a new luminous quality in oil paint by thinning the paint with turpentine. The colors soaked into the white canvas ground, decreasing the saturation of the hues and achieving an effect similar to the brightness of watercolors.

Unlike the single all-over texture that Pollock's drip method yields, Frankenthaler retains specific hues and shapes that float in an undefined space across the

FIGURE 72. HELEN FRANKENTHALER. *Mountains and Sea.* 1952. 86 3/8 x 117 1/4" (7' 2 3/8" x 9' 1/4"). Collection of the artist (on extended loan to the National Gallery of Art, Washington, D.C.).

picture surface. While one cannot actually identify water and mountains, one senses both the color and light of a landscape. These qualities, combined with the sheer scale of the piece, make the viewer feel immersed in a watery natural environment. Frankenthaler painted this work in New York after spending the summer in Nova Scotia. She recalled: "I came back and did *Mountains and Sea* and I know the landscapes were in my arms as I did it."[7]

The drips and splatters that occur all over the canvas indicate that the painting of the work was a highly spontaneous, almost uncontrolled act made visible in the finished work. However, there is a clear centering of the main mass, a controlled balance that belies the apparent spontaneity of the technique. The potentialities for the "soak-stain" technique were appreciated by two major artists, Morris Louis and Kenneth Noland, who proceeded to develop their own staining techniques in the late 1950s.

In 1963 Frankenthaler switched from oil paint to acrylics, which do not soak into the canvas as quickly as oils and therefore can be pushed or "flooded" over the surface. This method is apparent in *Flood* (Figure 73), painted in 1967, in which large areas of color sweep in irregular bands across almost 12 feet of canvas.

FIGURE 73.   HELEN FRANKENTHALER. *Flood.* 1967. Synthetic polymer. 124 x 140''. Collection of the Whitney Museum of American Art, New York. Gift of the Friends of the Whitney Museum of American Art.

Moving up from the bottom, there is a band of deep blue, then green, which continues up the right side. The "sky" is filled with swirling bands of mustard-yellow and hot pink. One can hardly help but read this image in terms of landscape, seeing a strip of water, land, and then an active sky, which rolls across the canvas. In the upper left, there is a dark area that seems to be an approaching storm. These associations are conveyed through the most minimal means available—colored shapes. But the colors and their shapes are so powerful and so precisely controlled that one reads them as forces of nature. The viewer is absorbed by the splendor of this scene, created on an immense scale, rivaling the scale of nature. Like Pollock and other painters of the 1950s and 1960s, Frankenthaler exploited the expressive possibilities of large-scale paintings.

Frankenthaler's contribution to the history of contemporary painting has long been recognized. In 1969 she was given a major retrospective at the Whitney Museum in New York. Her works reveal a unique color sensibility, an innovative method of paint application, and a personal imagery that conveys the beauty and vastness of nature in an abstract and non-descriptive, yet evocative, style.

LOUISE NEVELSON (1889–   )

Louise Nevelson is generally recognized as one of the major innovators in the history of twentieth-century sculpture. By the late 1950s, she was making large-scale works that were technically and formally without art historical precedents.

Louise Berliawsky was born in Russia to Jewish parents. When she was six years old, the family emigrated to the United States, settling in Rockland, Maine. Louise's affinity for wood dates from her childhood, spent in the proximity of her father's lumber yard. In 1920 she married Charles Nevelson, whose family owned a cargo-shipping business. Two years later her son Myron was born. During the 1920s, Nevelson studied voice, drama, and dance, as well as the visual arts. In 1931 she separated from her husband and began to focus her energies on her painting classes at the Art Students League. She continued her painting studies through the 1940s, but it was only when she began to make sculpture from pieces of wood, nailed together and painted a uniform color, that Nevelson found her identity as an artist. Her reputation rests upon a series of environmental structures that she began building in the 1950s.

These large-scale works are constructed from fragments of wood, arranged in compositions within box-like enclosures. They are always painted a uniform color. During the 1950s, the color was black, but later the color changed to white, then gold. However, the black sculptures are the best known and most characteristic of her works.

Sky Cathedral (Figure 74) is one wall of an environmental installation typical of her style. The work is over 8 feet tall and 11 feet wide. By its sheer scale, it dominates the viewer and commands attention. The title evokes a sense of the sculpture as mysterious, awe-inspiring architecture. It is not a unified, coherently

FIGURE 74. LOUISE NEVELSON. *Sky Cathedral*. 1958. Wood, painted black. 102 1/2 x 133 1/2''. Albright-Knox Art Gallery, Buffalo, New York. George B. and Jenny R. Mathews Fund, 1970.

designed work. In this sense, Nevelson's aesthetic is diametrically opposed to the sculptures of contemporary Minimalism. *Sky Cathedral* is divided into box-like enclosures so the work operates on two levels: an overall impression and the compositions of each individual box.

Nevelson began to enclose her sculpture in boxes in 1956 for emotional reasons:

> I wanted to be more secretive about the work and I began working in the enclosures. . . . There's something more private about it for me and gives me a better sense of security.[8]

From the confined limits of the box, Nevelson found the freedom to develop the fullest range of expressive potential in the interior compositions. However, she wanted to maintain a monumental scale for her sculpture so she began piling these boxes on top of one other to create larger scaled works:

> I attribute the walls to this: I had loads of energy. I mean, energy and energy and loads of creative energy. . . . So I began to stack my sculptures into an environment. It was natural. It was a flowing energy. I think there is something in the consciousness of the creative person that adds up, and the multiple image that I give, say, in an enormous wall gives me so much satisfaction. There is great satisfaction in seeing a splendid, big, enormous work of art.[9]

Part of the distinction of Nevelson's sculpture is that it operates very effectively on the microcosmic scale of the individual enclosures and the macrocosmic scale of a mural or piece of architecture.

Sky Cathedral contains great variety and diversity within its overall unity. Each of the enclosures has a distinctive composition, balanced and complete within its own confines. For example, the third box from the left, on the floor, is a study in curving versus straight elements. Two sweeping arcs are counterbalanced by four horizontal units. The circular shape is then repeated with a disk set on a third spatial level. It is very carefully arranged so that the abstract elements contain their own tensions. Unity is maintained by the overall black color and the consistency of the use of wood fragments.

Black is traditionally associated with death in our society. Yet Nevelson has said: ". . . it's only an assumption of the western world that it means death; for me it may mean finish, completeness, maybe eternity."[10]

Nevelson's art, as noted above, had variety and unity, complexity and a certain awesome simplicity. It is both very small and intimate in the box compositions and very large in overall impact. Nevelson believes that her work reflects her identity as a woman:

> I feel that my works are definitely feminine. . . . A man simply couldn't use the means of, say, fingerwork to produce my small pieces. They are like need-lework. . . . My work is delicate; it may look strong, but it is delicate. . . . My whole life is in it, and my whole life is feminine. . . . Women through all ages could have had physical strength and mental creativity and still have been feminine. The fact that these things have been suppressed is the fault of society.[11]

It may be surprising at first to hear Nevelson relate her work—which uses nails, saws, and other tools to needlework. But Nevelson has indeed taken bits and pieces of material, the debris of society, and transformed them, like a patchwork quilt, into a series of beautiful and impressive works of art, unlike the sculpture of any other creator.

AGNES MARTIN (1912–   )

Agnes Martin's mature works, which date from the early 1960s, concentrate on the use of a grid drawn in pencil on a luminous ground. Her paintings are early and characteristic examples of Minimalism, a movement that affected a number of artists in the 1960s. Reacting against the painterly emotionalism of Abstract Expressionism, Martin's extremely delicate, humble paintings are conceptually crystalline, eliminating any elements of chance or spontaneity in their execution. Her paintings are holistic because the entire surface is created through the repetition of module units. Martin's works were seminal influences for the next generation of artists, including Eva Hesse.

Martin was born on a wheat farm in Saskatchewan, Canada. Her father died while she was still very young, and the family moved to Vancouver. In 1941 Martin began attending Columbia University's Teachers College. By 1954 she had earned a B.S. and an M.A. degree in fine arts and arts administration at Columbia and was determined to become a painter. She was living in New York during the most active and formative era of Abstract Expressionism. After graduation from Columbia she moved to New Mexico, settling in Taos in 1956.

Martin's paintings of the early 1950s reveal the influence of Abstract Expressionist painters, such as Arshile Gorky and William Baziotes, through her use of biomorphic, abstract forms, which convey a symbolic or narrative content. By 1955 she was using geometric shapes placed on pale, luminous backgrounds. In 1957, with the support of the gallery owner Betty Parsons, Martin returned to New York. From this time onward, her works developed in the direction of increasing simplicity of structure and uniformity of surface. Her paintings either employ the repetition of a single form or the depiction of one large form.

By 1961 Martin was using the format of the grid on a square canvas. Her horizontal and vertical units created the effect of a veil suspended within the canvas edges. Her grids eventually expanded to cover the entire surface of the canvas, creating a total unity between the picture surface and the module. Martin's grids are usually subdivided into rectangular units. She explained her use of the rectangle in the following way:

> My formats are square, but the grids never are absolutely square, they are rectangles, a little bit off the square, making a sort of contradiction, a dissonance, though I didn't set out to do it that way. When I cover the square surface with rectangles, it lightens the weight of the square, destroys its power.[12]

Martin's characteristic use of pencil creates "channels of nuance stretched on a rack of linear tensions . . ."[13] As opposed to paint or ink, a pencil does not respond readily to the artist's hand pressure. Therefore, the selection of pencil as a medium is a reaction against the gestural painters of Abstract Expressionism.[14]

Although Martin has confined her art within a narrow set of limitations, there is great variety within the self-imposed confines of the grid. Her grids are never identical, but vary in proportions, size, and color. Furthermore, as Lawrence Alloway has noted, the selection of a conceptual order is just as personal as autographic tracks of the brush.[15]

In their accumulation of small, identical units, Martin's images evoke the sense of the sublimely infinite. They seem as if they could be extended indefinitely to infinity. "A collection of similar bits, beyond easy counting, implies infinity; that is why the internal area of a Martin painting can seem highly expansive."[16] They are intended to evoke a mystical, meditative response in the viewer.

Martin's images, then, are deceptively simple. While one can grasp her system almost instantly, the implications of her images are complex. It is paradoxical but accurate to see in Martin's highly structured and impersonal surfaces a visual metaphor for the vastness of the universe and the multiplicity existing within nature.

BRIDGET RILEY (1931–   )

Bridget Riley has received international recognition as one of the innovators in the Op Art movement. Her works concentrate on the dynamics of visual perception, the physiological core of the visual arts. Riley's paintings challenge the viewer to see in unaccustomed ways.

Born in London, Riley received her early training at Goldsmith's School of Art and at the Painting School of the Royal College of Art. She left school with no personal sense of direction and did very little painting until 1959. In that year she became interested in Georges Seurat, the theories of pointillism, and the art of the Italian Futurists. By 1961 Riley had focused her energies on the creation of images in black and white in which basic units are altered to create a visual effect of motion. Unlike Martin, who maintains a uniformity in her grids, Riley's painting explores the effects of variations in regular patterning. In 1961 she saw works by Victor Vasarely for the first time. Encouraged by this artist's example, she pursued her interests in the optical ''tricks'' that can be achieved through the manipulation of geometric shapes.

Fall (Figure 75) is a square canvas in which black and white lines of equal

FIGURE 75. BRIDGET RILEY. *Fall*. 1963. Emulsion on board. 55 1/2 x 55 1/2''. The Tate Gallery, London. Reproduced by permission of the artist.

width undulate from top to bottom. Toward the bottom, the "visual frequency" (Riley's term) changes from the slow, even curves of the upper two-thirds of the canvas to shorter, more rapid undulations. The eye tries to mix the black and white lines unsuccessfully and perceives pulsations of gray. An almost painfully intense visual vibration results. As William Seitz observed: "The eyes seem to be bombarded with pure energy."[17] The image creates an illusion of movement. We feel as if these lines are actually moving through space. There is also a sense of sound waves, and the analogy to musical rhythms is unavoidable.

Riley's *Fall* and other Op Art paintings sacrifice narrative content and the entire Western tradition of optical illusion. There are few precedents for images that focus so exclusively on the way we see. Riley's creative input for this work resides in the selection of the unit sizes and in the changes in those units to alter the visual rhythm of the painting. As opposed to Frankenthaler's paintings, which reveal the technical skill and manual expertise of the artist, Riley's surfaces, like Martin's, are smooth and immaculate.

Riley participated in the seminal exhibition that defined and illustrated the artistic movement since named Op Art. "The Responsive Eye" opened at New York's Museum of Modern Art in 1965 with a reproduction of Riley's *Current* (1964) on the cover of the catalogue. Her paintings, then limited to black and white, elicited wide critical and popular success.

In the late 1960s, Riley incorporated color into her systemic images. Retaining the use of repeating geometric units, her subtle color variations create beautiful and intriguing effects of movement. Her formative contribution to Op Art has long been recognized, and in 1971 she was given a major retrospective exhibition at the Hayward Gallery in London.

EVA HESSE (1936–1970)

Eva Hesse's mature and significant career as an artist is concentrated within the brief span of five years, 1966 through 1970, the year she died from a brain tumor at the age of thirty-four. During this time, she created a number of sculptures that differ in many ways from the prevailing contemporary aesthetic of Minimalism. As a post-Minimalist, Hesse's works were formally, technically and conceptually innovative and influential for the direction of sculpture during the 1970s. Her oeuvre is well documented and her contribution to the history of contemporary art is widely recognized.

Hesse was born in Hamburg into a German Jewish family. She and her sister escaped extermination in the Holocaust by leaving Germany on a children's train bound for neutral Holland. Her parents rejoined them several months later, and the family settled in New York City in 1939. New traumas came when her parents were divorced and when, the following year, her mother committed suicide. By age sixteen, Hesse had decided to become an artist. She studied at several New York art schools: Pratt Institute, the Art Students League, and Cooper Union. From 1957 to 1959, Hesse attended Yale University's School of Art and Architecture.

Returning to New York City, she integrated herself into the avant-garde art community. In 1961 she married the artist Tom Doyle, and in 1964 the couple spent a year in Germany. During this stay abroad, Hesse abandoned painting and started making three-dimensional, biomorphic reliefs, related in form and spirit to Surrealism.

In 1966 two emotionally traumatic events occurred in Hesse's life: Her marriage ended and her father died. She emerged from these crises a mature sculptor with a personal style and direction. That same year she participated, along with Louise Bourgeois, in a group show called "Eccentric Abstraction," curated by Lucy Lippard. This exhibition first defined the post-Minimal attitude of a group of contemporary sculptors.

Hesse shared with Claus Oldenburg, Robert Smithson, Lucas Samaras, and Louise Bourgeois an aversion to the architectural and "serious" sculptural ambitions of Minimalism. Hesse was one of the first artists to use a wide range of non-traditional materials to make her objects. Her earliest works were made from limp and pliable materials, such as cord, rubber tubing, or wire, emerging from boards mounted on a wall. Hesse's works often employed the repetition of non-identical module units. She was very aware and deliberate about her intentions. In the last year of her life she told an interviewer:

> If something is meaningful, maybe it's more meaningful said ten times. It's not just an esthetic choice. If something is absurd, it's much more absurd if it's repeated . . . repetition does enlarge or increase or exaggerate an idea or purpose in a statement.[18]

In 1967 Hesse made *Repetition Nineteen,* in which nineteen nearly identical buckets are scattered about the floor. That same year, she discovered latex rubber, a sensuous and flexible but impermanent material. The following year she also began working with fiberglass.

These interests are all apparent in *Vinculum I* (Figure 76), created in the last year of her life, when she was quite ill. This piece consists of two ladders made of irregularly shaped fiberglass units. The two forms are joined by rubber tubing strung horizontally between them and tumbling down loosely on the floor. A "vinculum" is defined as a connecting bond or tie. In mathematics, it is a horizontal line placed over two or more members of a compound quantity to show that they are to be treated together. Thus, the rubber tubing in this work forms a vinculum between the grid units, both formally and in the literal sense of tying or binding the two units together.

Vinculum I is typical of Hesse's creations in that it incorporates formal opposites: the hard fiberglass units contrasting with the soft and pliable rubber tubes. Hesse had this to say about her use of opposites:

> . . . absurdity is the key word. . . . It has to do with contradictions and oppositions. In the forms I use in my work, the contradictions are certainly there. I was always aware that I should take order versus chaos, stringy versus mass, huge versus small, and I would try to find the most absurd opposites or extreme opposites. . . . I was

FIGURE   76. EVA   HESSE. *Vinculum I.* 1969. Fiberglass, rubber tubing, metal screen. 8' x 8'' x 2'. Collection of Mr. and Mrs. Victor W. Ganz.

always aware of their absurdity and also their formal contradictions, and it was always more interesting than making something average, normal, right size, right proportion. . . .[19]

The use of rubber tubing and fiberglass materials for the creation of sculpture is extremely innovative. Another innovation is the way this work simply leans against the wall. Hesse's objects often hover ambiguously between two-dimensional painting and three-dimensional sculpture. This work is quite flat and the tubing is very linear. It cannot stand by itself—it must lean against the wall, yet it is neither a painting nor a relief, artistic forms which are usually hung on a wall.

The sculpture of Eva Hesse challenges many traditional attitudes concerning our expectations of the appearance of a piece of sculpture and the materials used in its construction. In a witty and understated way, Hesse's works are revolutionary, transforming the medium and the intellectual approach to the creation of a work of "art."

LOUISE BOURGEOIS (1911–   )

Since the late 1940s, Louise Bourgeois has created works of sculpture that express a highly personal symbolic system. Unaffected by the successive art movements that have dominated the art world since World War II, she has pursued personal goals, tenaciously seeking formal equivalents for the constants underlying the human condition. Working in a wide variety of media, ranging from traditional sculptural materials, such as marble, wood, and bronze, to impermanent latex, Bourgeois' works explore the relationship between man and woman and the concept of androgyny, as well as seeking equivalents for emotional states.

Bourgeois was born in France into a family in which her artistic talents were not only recognized but put to use. Her parents repaired Aubusson tapestries, and her job as a child was to draw in the missing parts to guide the weavers. She received a classical education at the Sorbonne, where she studied philosophy and geometry. She also studied art history at the Ecole du Louvre. She acquired academic training in the fine arts at the Ecole des Beaux-Arts, which she attended from 1936 to 1938. She moved to New York in 1938 and has lived there ever since.

In the late 1940s, Bourgeois created simple wooden structures that convey a powerful and eerie presence. *The Blind Leading the Blind* consists of a double row of upright wooden posts that taper to pointed "feet." The posts are connected by an irregularly shaped lintel. The almost uniform uprights are easily interpreted as anonymous, unindividualized persons. The lintel binds them together, turning the separate posts into an architectural structure. Painted black, like Nevelson's later constructions, the work conveys a sense of monotonous menace. It is interesting and relevant that this work was created during the McCarthy Era, around the time when Bourgeois, Duchamp, and other artists were being investigated by the House Committee on Un-American Activities. It reflects the paranoia about Communism that had temporarily seized the government machinery of the United States.

Bourgeois has continued to explore the theme of uniformity versus individuality in both wood and marble constructions. *Eye to Eye* (Figure 77) consists of a cluster of marble units of varying heights. A work such as this evokes, on an abstract, symbolic level, the congestion of human society. In the highly compressed grouping of forms and the diversity within their unity, one can see a metaphor for the relationship of the individual or the family to the society as a whole.

The use of a group of regular units is also seen in Bourgeois' *Cumulus* series from the late 1960s. In these works, most of which are carved in marble, rounded forms seem to be bursting through or growing out of undifferentiated matter. Like spores emerging from a sac, or a penis becoming erect, these rounded forms, which also could be interpreted as breast shapes, are symbols of a life force. They evoke a sense of eclosion and androgynous generation.

In her most recent works, such as *Le Trani Episode* (Figure 78), Bourgeois creates simple shapes, on a relatively small scale, that condense the essence of male and female sexual distinctions into one consolidated form. *Le Trani Episode* consists of two objects resting one on top of the other. The upper form is an elongated bulbous shape with a nipple at one end. The lower form, although very similar, is more elongated and is pointed on both ends. These shapes evoke the forms of both a female breast and a partially erect penis. The use of latex, textured like flesh on the surface, further emphasizes the organic qualities of the image. In *Le Trani*

FIGURE 77. LOUISE BOURGEOIS. *Eye to Eye.* c. 1970. Marble. 31 1/2'' high x 29 7/8'' diameter. Photograph © Helaine Messer. Private collection, New York.

Episode, Bourgeois uncovers the formal resemblances beneath the sexually differentiated anatomy of male and female, expressing the concept of androgyny.

Bourgeois' works do not fit within a stylistic movement or a neatly defined category. She has worked in a wide variety of media, and in a range of different styles, adjusting her formal means to fit her expressive intent. She deals with the most fascinating questions of the human spirit—the relationship between the sexes and the relationship of the individual and the society in which he or she lives. Honored with a major retrospective of her works at the Museum of Modern Art in 1982, Bourgeois' contribution to the history of sculpture is only recently being fully appreciated.

AFRO-AMERICAN ARTISTS

The Afro-American women who have aspired to become artists have suffered under the double oppression and discrimination of being both black and female. While a few black men managed to surmount the obstacles of race to become competent professionals in the nineteenth century, Edmonia Lewis (one of the ''Marmorean

FIGURE 78. LOUISE BOURGEOIS. *Le Trani Episode*. c. 1971–72. Hydrocal and latex. 16 1/2 x 23 1/8 x 23 1/4''. Photograph: Peter Moore. Private collection, New York. Reproduced by permission of the artist.

Flock'' discussed in Chapter 7) was the only black woman who achieved professional success and a high level of technical expertise.

In the twentieth century, many Afro-American women have pursued artistic careers worthy of recognition. Alma Thomas, for example, is known for elegant abstractions based on her perceptions of landscape. These works are lovely and lyrical but impossible to identify as the creation of an Afro-American. Beginning in the 1960s, a group of Afro-American artists developed styles and subjects identifiable with the special concerns of American blacks. Many artists expressed their attitudes toward racial discrimination and oppression in their works.

Bettye Saar (1926–   )

Bettye Saar is one noted artist who developed a personal style to convey her distinctive vision outside the realm of the ''fine arts'' and the traditions of Western art. Born in Los Angeles, she studied art at Pasadena City College, graduating in 1949. During the 1950s, she raised a family, but in the 1960s she began making constructions in boxes. Inspired by the works of Joseph Cornell, Saar gathered together objects, fabrics, and other bits and pieces with which she composed her imaginative tableaux. Using this assemblage technique, Saar discovered the formal means by which she could best express a personal content. In the mid-1960s and early 1970s, Saar focused on the ready-made stereotypes of black people promoted by white society to make her political statements. In some works she used "Uncle Tom" or "Little Black Sambo" or "Aunt Jemima." In *The Liberation of Aunt Jemima* (Figure 79), Saar explodes the myth of the "good house nigger."[20] Aunt Jemima holds a broom in one hand and a rifle in the other. The anger and violence of the black revolution is here given a forceful symbol.

Faith Ringgold (1930–   )

Faith Ringgold is an artist of impressive talents who also developed her personal style outside the Western Renaissance tradition. Born in Harlem, Ringgold studied art at the City College of New York. Like Saar, Ringgold's education was

FIGURE 79. BETTYE SAAR. *The Liberation of Aunt Jemima*. 1972. Mixed media. 11 3/4 x 8 x 2 3/4'' (29.8 x 20.2 x 6.8 cm.). University Art Museum, University of California, Berkeley, Ca. Purchased with the aid of funds from the National Endowment for the Arts (Selected by the Committee for the Acquisition of Afro-American Art). (UAM 1972.84)

acquired through the subsidized public schools for higher education. In the mid 1960s, inspired by the political upheavals of the civil rights movement, Ringgold painted a 12-foot wide mural entitled *Die* (Figure 80). Using flat, unmodulated colors, Ringgold achieves a decorative and original style for a vision of interracial violence. While black and white adults attack each other, two children huddle together in the center of the composition hoping to survive the massacre.

Ringgold recalls that she became a feminist in 1970, when she launched a protest against an all-male exhibition at the School of Visual Arts in New York, in itself designed to protest war, racism, and sexism. Ringgold's feminism became incorporated into her art in 1973, when she abandoned oil painting and began making soft sculpture using sewing and other craft techniques. Her mother had been a fashion designer, and Ringgold recalls that when she was young her mother was always sewing. However, it was the feminist movement that sanctioned her use of these techniques for the creation of art. "If I'd been left alone, I'd have done my own kind of thing earlier, based on sewing. As it was, it wasn't until the Women's Movement that I got the go-ahead to do that kind of work."[21] During this time she had been teaching African crafts, such as beadwork, appliqué, and mask-making, at the Bank Street College in New York. Combining this interest in African crafts with her feminist consciousness of traditional women's art, she decided to make soft sculptures based on her memory images of black people. The results are the group of works known collectively as the *Family of Women* (Figure 81). Using a variety of techniques, needlepoint, braided ribbon, beading, and sewn fabric, these images are imaginative presences with foam bodies. They are dressed in African-inspired clothing and the sewn faces are derived from African masks.

FIGURE 80. FAITH RINGGOLD. *Die.* 1967. Oil on canvas. 72 x 144''. Photo by Malcolm Varon, N.Y.C. Reproduced by permission of the artist.

FIGURE 81. FAITH RING-GOLD. *Mama Jones, Andrew, Barbara, and Faith.* 1973. Mixed media, life size. From *The Family of Women* series. Photo by Faith Ringgold. Reproduced by permission of the artist.

Drawing on her heritage as both an Afro-American and a woman, Ringgold has evolved a set of original images that speak directly of her personal experiences.

AUDREY FLACK (1931–   )

Audrey Flack is one of the originators and most prominent artists in the 1970s movement known as Photo Realism. Like Don Eddy and Richard Estes, Flack uses photographic reproductions, i.e., color slides, projected onto the canvas to create her paintings. However, while Eddy and Estes merely select their subjects from the urban environment, Flack's paintings are wholly artificial still life arrangements. Her choice of objects and their juxtapositions and relative sizes are totally controlled by the artist. Her paintings always convey a precise message, sometimes with a biographical content, at other times with public or political significance.

Flack, like Frankenthaler and Ringgold, was born in New York. She studied at the High School of Music and Art, where she was trained in the Cubist idiom. At Cooper Union, where the prevailing style was Abstract Expressionism, Flack absorbed the lessons of the gesture painters. She attended Yale University's Graduate School and continued her studies of the figure at the Art Students League. In the mid-1950s, Flack was one of the very few artists who displayed paintings of the human figure. Abstraction so dominated the art world at that time that her realistic art was little appreciated. Nevertheless, she persisted in retaining recognizable subjects in her art through the 1960s. The *Kennedy Motorcade* (1964) was the first painting in which she used a color photograph as a reference.[22] Thereafter, she continued to use photographs as sources for her paintings and in the early 1970s discovered the advantages of using a color slide projected directly on the canvas. In this way, she could increase the scale and achieve greater brilliance of color in her canvases.

Flack's characteristic paintings from the 1970s use an airbrush to create an immaculate surface that can imitate the textures of objects. She layers the three primary hues in transparent glazes so the colors are mixed optically. In this way, she eliminates line and brushstrokes but retains a precision useful for the description of a variety of reflective surfaces.

One of her most impressive and famous paintings is *World War II, April 1945* (Figure 82), referring to the liberation of the Nazi concentration camp at Buchenwald. As a source for her painting, Flack employs Bourke-White's photo *The Living Dead of Buchenwald* (see Figure 67). She combines Bourke-White's document with other still life objects to create an image that is both a tribute to the survivors and a memorial to the six million Jews who died in the Holocaust. The single rose, burning candle, and black border are readily recognized symbols for commemorating the dead. The watch, butterfly, and overripe pear are additional references to mortality. The printed statement in the lower right-hand corner is a rabbinical quotation affirming faith in God: ''You can take everything from me—the pillow from under my head, my house—but you cannot take God from my heart.'' The dripping red wax from the candle looks like blood staining the photo. The cakes are almost obscene sensual indulgences compared with the deprivation the concentration camp victims endured. Thus, each carefully selected object adds another layer of meaning to the image.

The airbrushed surface of the painting conveys the variety of textures of the objects. Like other realists, Flack is interested in surfaces that reflect light, such as the silver tray and candlestick, the teacup, and the blue glass chalice. Each object is so large, however, that one does not truly recognize them as ''real.'' Like O'Keeffe, Flack understands the power of a close-up vision. Seeing a small object very enlarged, the viewer is compelled to look carefully at that object. In this work, Flack has adapted the heroic scale of Abstract Expressionism and color field painting to her still life composition.

There is no table surface and no defined perspective space. The high viewpoint

FIGURE 82. AUDREY FLACK. *World War II, April 1945*. 1976–77. Acrylic and oil on canvas. 96 x 96'', incorporating a portion of the Margaret Bourke-White photograph ''Buchenwald, 1945'' copyright Time Inc. Photograph courtesy Louis K. Meisel Gallery.

flattens the space, bringing each object close to us. The colors are harsh, dominated by highly saturated primaries, red, blue, and yellow. They are uncomfortable to look at, reinforcing the unpleasant content of the image. One critic has summed up the impact of *World War II, April 1945* as ''a painting that is difficult to forget.''[23]

Since the revived appreciation in the 1970s for paintings with recognizable subjects, Flack's originality and talent have received critical and popular attention. One of her paintings was the first Photo Realist work purchased by the Museum of Modern Art in New York.

Notes

INTRODUCTION

1. Ann Sutherland Harris and Linda Nochlin, *Women Artists: 1550–1950* (New York: Alfred A. Knopf, 1977), p. 29.
2. Rozsika Parker and Griselda Pollack, *Old Mistresses: Women, Art, and Ideology* (New York: Pantheon Books, 1981), pp. 44–45.

CHAPTER 1

1. Joseph Campbell, *The Masks of God: Primitive Mythology* (New York: Viking Press, 1959), p. 313.
2. Paula Webster, "Matriarchy: A Vision of Power," in Rayna R. Reiter, *Toward an Anthropology of Women* (New York and London: Monthly Review Press, 1975), p. 143.
3. Ann Oakley, *Sex, Gender and Society* (New York: Harper and Row, 1972), p. 165.
4. Ruby Rohrlich-Leavitt, "Women in Transition: Crete and Sumer," in Renate Bridenthal and Claudia Koonz (eds.), *Becoming Visible: Women in European History* (Boston: Houghton Mifflin, 1977), p. 40.
5. Eleanor Leacock, "Women in Egalitarian Societies," in *Becoming Visible,* p. 17.
6. Rayna R. Reiter, "Men and Women in the South of France: Public and Private Domains," in *Toward an Anthropology of Women,* pp. 252–82.
7. For the following discussion I have relied on Ilse Seibert, *Women in the Ancient Near East,* trans. Marianne Herzfeld (New York: Abner Schram, 1974).
8. The seal is reproduced in Seibert, *Women in the Ancient Near East,* p. 22.
9. Sarah B. Pomeroy, *Goddesses, Whores, Wives and Slaves: Women in Classical Antiquity* (New York: Schocken Books, 1975), p. 227.
10. Sarah B. Pomeroy, "A Classical Scholar's Perspective on Matriarchy," in Berenice A. Carroll (ed.), *Liberating Women's History: Theoretical and Critical Essays* (Urbana: University of Illinois Press, 1976), p. 220, 223.

11. Pomeroy, *Goddesses, Whores, Wives and Slaves*, pp. 64–78.
12. Kate McK. Elderkin, "The Contribution of Women to Ornament in Antiquity," in *Classical Studies Presented to Edward Capps on his Seventieth Birthday* (Princeton: Princeton University Press, 1936), p. 125.
13. Pomeroy, *Goddesses, Whores, Wives and Slaves*, p. 125.
14. Elderkin, "The Contribution of Women to Ornament," pp. 125–26.
15. Giovanni Boccaccio, *Concerning Famous Women*, trans. with an introduction by Guido A. Guarino (New Brunswick: Rutgers University Press, 1963), p. 131.
16. Robert Rosenblum, "The Origin of Painting: A Problem in the Iconography of Romantic Classicism," *Art Bulletin* 39 (1957), pp. 279–82.
17. These histories include: Ernest Guhl, *Die Frauen in der Kunstgeschichte* (Berlin, 1858); Elizabeth Fries Lummis Ellet, *Women Artists in All Ages and Countries* (New York, 1859); Octave Fidière, *Les Femmes artistes à l' Académie royale de peinture et de sculpture* (Paris, 1885); Walter Sparrow, *Women Painters of the World* (London, 1905).
18. Verena Zinserling, *Women in Greece and Rome*, trans. L. A. Jones (New York: Abner Schram, 1973), p. 64.
19. Herlihy notes that there were fewer girls reaching adulthood than boys, but he does not attribute this directly to female infanticide. David Herlihy, "Life Expectancies for Women in Medieval Society," in Rosemarie Thee Morewedge (ed.), *The Role of Women in the Middle Ages* (Albany: The State University of New York Press, 1975), pp. 4–5.
20. JoAnn McNamara and Suzanne Wemple, "The Power of Women Through the Family in Medieval Europe: 500–1100," in Mary Hartman and Louise Banner (eds.), *Clio's Consciousness Raised* (New York: Harper Colophon Books, 1974), pp. 103–4.
21. Pomeroy, *Goddesses, Whores, Wives and Slaves*, pp. 199–200.
22. Zinserling, *Women in Greece and Rome*, p. 58.
23. Pliny, the Elder, *Naturalis Historia*, 147, trans. K. Jex-Black and E. Sellers, *The Elder Pliny's Chapters on the History of Art* (Chicago: Argonaut,1968, photocopy of 1896 edition), p. 171.

CHAPTER 2

1. Susan Mosher Stuard, ed., *Women in Medieval Society* (Philadelphia: The University of Pennsylvania Press, 1977), p. 9.
2. JoAnn McNamara and Suzanne F. Wemple, "Sanctity and Power," in *Women in Medieval Society* p. 108.
3. Eileen Power, *Medieval Women*, ed. M. M. Postan (London: Cambridge University Press, 1975), p. 20.
4. F. Heer, *The Medieval World: Europe 1100–1350* (London: Weidenfeld and Nicolson, 1962), p. 265.
5. Brenda M. Bolton, "Mulieres Sanctae," in *Women in Medieval Society*, pp. 45–47.
6. Dorothy Miner, *Anastaise and Her Sisters* (Baltimore: Walters Art Gallery, 1974), pp. 10–11.
7. *Ibid.*, p. 10.
8. Annemarie Weyl Carr, "Women Artists in the Middle Ages," *Feminist Art Journal* V, no. 1 (1976), p. 6.
9. Power, *Medieval Women*, p. 38.
10. *Ibid.*, pp. 87–88.

11. Sibylle Harksen, *Women in the Middle Ages,* trans. Marianne Herzfeld (New York: Abner Schram, 1975), p. 28.

12. Kathleen Casey, "The Cheshire Cat: Reconstructing the Experience of Medieval Women," in *Liberating Women's History,* p. 247, note 7.

13. Millard Meiss, *French Painting in the Time of Jean de Berry* (London: Phaidon, 1967–68), I, p. 3.

14. Dorothy Miner believes that Le Noir is identical with the artist identified by Meiss as the "Passion Master" (see *Anastaise and Her Sisters,* p. 19). While Meiss accepts the possibility that Le Noir might be the name of the artist whose works form a stylistic group, he uses the name "Passion Master" for this figure, stopping short of attributing these works to Jean Le Noir (*French Painting,* pp. 167–68).

15. Miner, *Anastaise and Her Sisters,* pp. 18–19.

16. A. G. I. Christie, *English Medieval Embroidery* (Oxford: Clarendon Press, 1938), p. 1.

17. Christie, *English Medieval Embroidery,* Appendix I.

18. The most complete discussion of the Bayeux Tapestry is in F. Stenton (ed.), *The Bayeux Tapestry* (London: Phaidon, 1957).

19. Harris and Nochlin, *Women Artists: 1550–1950,* pp. 16–17.

CHAPTER 3

1. E. William Monter, "The Pedestal and the Stake: Courtly Love and Witchcraft," in *Becoming Visible,* p.133.

2. Louise A. Tilly and Joan W. Scott, *Women, Work, and Family* (New York: Holt, Rinehart and Winston, 1978), p. 60.

3. Joan Kelly-Gadol, "Did Women Have a Renaissance?" in *Becoming Visible,* pp. 160–61.

4. J. O'Faolain and L. Martines, *Not in God's Image* (New York: Harper and Row, 1973), p. 145.

5. Hannelore Sachs, *The Renaissance Woman,* trans. Marianne Herzfeld (New York: McGraw-Hill, 1971), p. 9.

6. Ruth Kelso, *Doctrine for the Lady of the Renaissance* (Urbana: University of Illinois Press, 1956), pp. 59, 77.

7. Monter,"The Pedestal and the Stake," p. 127.

8. Sherrin Marshall Wyntjes, "Women in the Reformation Era," in *Becoming Visible,* p. 186.

CHAPTER 4

1. Charles de Tolnay, "Sofonisba Anguissola and Her Relations with Michelangelo," *Journal of the Walters Art Gallery* IV (1941), pp. 115–19.

2. Eleanor Tufts, *Our Hidden Heritage: Five Centuries of Women Artists* (New York and London: Paddington Press, 1974), p. 21.

3. Mario Praz, *Conversation Pieces: A Survey of the Informal Group Portrait in Europe and America* (University Park and London: Pennsylvania State University Press, 1971), p. 149.

4. Mary Garrard, "Artemisia Gentileschi's *Self-Portrait as the Allegory of Painting,*" *Art Bulletin* (1980), p. 109.

CHAPTER 5

1.   Madlyn Millner Kahr, *Dutch Painting in the Seventeenth Century* (New York: Harper and Row, Icon Editions, 1978), p. ix.
2.   *Ibid.*, pp. 79–82.
3.   For a complete discussion of this painting, see Frima Fox Hofrichter, "Judith Leyster's *Proposition*—Between Vice and Virtue," *Feminist Art Journal* (1975), pp. 22–26. This essay is reprinted in Norma Broude and Mary Garrard, *Feminism and Art History: Questioning the Litany* (New York: Harper and Row, Icon Editions, 1982), pp. 173–83.
4.   Harris and Nochlin, *Women Artists: 1550–1959*, p. 154.
5.   Wilfred Blunt, *The Art of Botanical Illustration* (London: Collins, 1950), p. 128.

CHAPTER 6

1.   Harris and Nochlin, *Women Artists: 1550–1950*, p. 161.
2.   Tufts, *Our Hidden Heritage*, p. 110.
3.   Harris and Nochlin, *Women Artists: 1550–1950*, p. 183.
4.   For a thorough discussion of this painting, see Joseph Baillio, "*Marie-Antoinette et ses enfants* par Mme. Vigée-Lebrun," *L'Oeil* (March-April 1981).

CHAPTER 7

1.   Nicolai Cikovsky, *The White Marmorean Flock: Nineteenth Century American Neoclassical Sculptors* (Poughkeepsie, NY: Vassar College Art Gallery, 1974), catalogue entry on Zenobia, no page number.
2.   William H. Gerdts, *American Neoclassical Scultpure: The Marble Resurrection* (New York: Viking Press, 1973), p. 47.

CHAPTER 8

1.   Renate Bridenthal, "Something Old, Something New: Women Between the Two World Wars," in *Becoming Visible* pp. 440–41.
2.   Tilly and Scott, *Women, Work, and Family*, p. 77.
3.   *Ibid.*, p. 161.
4.   Alice Kessler-Harris, "Women, Work, and the Social Order," in *Liberating Women's History*, pp. 339–40.
5.   For a discussion of Enlightenment ideas on women's equality, see Katherine B. Clinton, "*Femme et philosophe:* Enlightenment Origins of Feminism," *Eighteenth-Century Studies* VIII, no. 3 (1975), 295ff. See also Abby R. Kleinbaum, "Women in the Age of Light," in *Becoming Visible*, pp. 217–35.
6.   Theodore Zeldin, *Oxford History of Modern Europe: France: 1848–1945* (Oxford: Clarendon Press, 1973) I, pp. 343–44.

CHAPTER 9

1. Wendy Slatkin, "Women Artists and the Ecole des Beaux-Arts: A Study of Institutional Change in Late Nineteenth-Century France." See also J. Diane Radycki, "The Life of Lady Art Students: Changing Art Education at the Turn of the Century," *Art Journal* vol. 42, no. 1 (Spring 1982), pp. 9–13.
2. Christine Jones Huber, *The Pennsylvania Academy and Its Women* (Philadelphia: The Pennsylvania Academy of Fine Arts, 1974).
3. Gabriel Weisberg, *The Realist Tradition: French Painting and Drawing, 1830–1900* (Cleveland: Cleveland Museum of Art, 1980), p. 1.
4. Anna Elizabeth Klumpke, *Rosa Bonheur, sa vie, son oeuvre* (Paris: Flammarion, 1908), pp. 311–12 (author's translation).
5. Theodore Stanton, ed., *Reminiscences of Rosa Bonheur* (London: 1910; rpt. New York: Hacker Art Books, 1976), p. 72.
6. Denis Rouart, *The Correspondence of Berthe Morisot* (London: Lund Humphries, 1957), p. 98.
7. *Ibid.*, p. 14.
8. Adylyn Breeskin, *Mary Cassatt: A Catalogue Raisonné of the Oils, Pastels, Watercolors and Drawings* (Washington, DC: Smithsonian Institution Press, 1970), p. 9.
9. Gillian Perry, *Paula Modersohn-Becker: Her Life and Work* (London: The Woman's Press, 1979), p. 115.

CHAPTER 10

1. Radycki, "The Life of Lady Art Students," p. 11.
2. Martha Kearns, *Käthe Kollwitz: Woman and Artist* (Old Westbury, NY: The Feminist Press, 1976), p. 192.
3. Margit Rowell and Angelica Zander Rudenstine, *Art of the Avant-Garde in Russia: Selections from the George Costakis Collection* (New York: The Solomon R. Guggenheim Museum, 1981), p. 23.
4. Camilla Gray, *The Russian Experiment in Art: 1863–1922* (New York: Abrams, 1972), p. 224.
5. Arthur A. Cohen, *Sonia Delaunay* (New York: Abrams, 1975), p. 61.
6. *Ibid.*, p. 83.
7. The following section on the Women of Surrealism was written by Janet Kaplan, Moore College of Art, Philadelphia, Pa.
8. Andre Breton, *Arcane 17,* quoted in Whitney Chadwick, "Eros or Thanatos—The Surrealist Cult of Love Reexamined," *Artforum,* 14 (November 1975), p. 50.
9. Gloria F. Orenstein, "Art History and the Case for the Women of Surrealism," *The Journal of General Education* XXVII, no. 1 (Spring 1975); reprinted in *Feminist Collage: Educating Women in the Visual Arts,* Judy Loeb (ed.) (New York: Teacher's College Press, Columbia University, 1979), pp. 35–59.
10. Josephine Withers, "The Famous Fur-Lined Teacup and the Anonymous Meret Oppenheim," *ARTS Magazine* vol. 52, no. 3 (November 1977), p. 88.
11. From *Chronicle* (1958), quoted in Withers, "The Famous Fur-Lined Teacup," p. 93.
12. For a discussion of the journey as a major theme in Varo's work, see Janet Kaplan, "Remedios Varo: Voyages and Visions," *Woman's Art Journal* vol. 1, no. 2 (Fall 1980/Winter 1981), pp. 13–18.

13. Quoted in Walter Gruen, "Index of Illustrations," *Remedios Varo,* with texts by Octavio Paz, Roger Cailliois, and Juliana Gonzalez (Mexico City: ERA Ediciones, 1966), p. 173.

14. Dorothea Tanning, in *XX^{e}Siècle* (September 1976), reprinted in the exhibition catalogue, *Dorothea Tanning: 10 Recent Paintings and a Biography* (New York: Gimpel-Weitzenhoffer Gallery, 1979), no page number.

15. O'Keeffe has refused permission to reproduce any of her paintings in this text. *Black Iris* and *Red Hills and Bones* appear in her book *Georgia O'Keeffe* (New York: Viking Press, 1976).

16. Georgia O'Keeffe exhibition catalogue, *An American Place, 1939,* reprinted in *Georgia O'Keeffe,* no page number.

17. Lloyd Goodrich and Doris Bry, *Georgia O'Keeffe* (New York: Whitney Museum of American Art, 1970), p. 18.

18. O'Keeffe exhibition catalogue, *An American Place, 1939,* no page number.

19. *Ibid.*

20. Roger Fry, quoted in *The Cameron Collection/Julia Margaret Cameron,* introduction by Colin Ford (New York: Van Nostrand Reinhold, 1975), p. 136.

21. William Innes Homer, *A Pictorial Heritage: The Photographs of Gertrude Käsebier* (Wilmington: Deleware Art Museum, 1979), p. 6.

22. Karin Becker Ohrn, *Dorothea Lange and the Documentary Tradition* (Baton Rouge: Louisiana State University Press, 1980), p. 79.

23. Margaret Bourke-White, *Dear Fatherland, Rest Quietly* (New York: Simon and Schuster, 1946), p. 73.

CHAPTER 11

1. Paul Guth, "Encounter with Germaine Richier," *Yale French Studies* vols. 19–20 (Spring 1957-Winter 1958), p. 80.

2. *Ibid.,* p. 82.

3. Erich Neumann, *The Great Mother: An Analysis of the Archetype,* trans. Ralph Manheim (New York: Pantheon Books, Bollingen Series XLVII, 1955), p. 127.

4. Guth, "Encounter with Germaine Richier," p. 83.

5. Barbara Hepworth, *A Pictorial Autobiography* (London: A. Zwemmer, 1959), p. 9.

6. Herbert Read, *Barbara Hepworth, Carvings and Drawings* (London: Lund Humphries, 1952), no page number.

7. Barbara Rose, *Helen Frankenthaler* (New York: Abrams, 1971), p. 54.

8. Quoted in Laurie Wilson, "Bride of the Black Moon: An Iconographic Study of the Work of Louise Nevelson," *ARTS Magazine* 54 (May 1980), p. 144.

9. Louise Nevelson, *Louise Nevelson: Atmospheres and Environments* (New York: C. N. Potter in association with the Whitney Museum of American Art, 1980), p. 77.

10. Wilson, "Bride of the Black Moon," p. 145.

11. Arnold B. Glimcher, *Louise Nevelson* (New York: Praeger, 1972), pp. 22–23.

12. Lucy Lippard, "Hommage to the Square," *Art in America* (July-August 1967), p. 55; quoted in *Agnes Martin* exhibition catalogue (Institute of Contemporary Art, University of Pennsylvania, 1973), p. 9.

13. Lucy Lippard, *From the Center: Feminist Essays of Women's Art* (New York: E. P. Dutton, 1976), p. 65.

14. Martin's lines are so faint that the grid is not legible in reproductions. For this reason, no example of her work has been included in this text.

15. Lawrence Alloway, "Systemic Painting," in Gregory Battcock (ed.) *Minimal Art: A Critical Anthology* (New York: E. P. Dutton, 1968), p. 55.

16. Lawrence Alloway, *Agnes Martin* exhibition catalogue (Philadelphia, Pa.: Institute of Contemporary Art, 1973), p. 10.

17. William C. Seitz, *The Responsive Eye* (New York: Museum of Modern Art, 1965), p. 31.

18. Cindy Nemser, "An Interview with Eva Hesse," *Artforum* (May 1970), p. 62.

19. *Ibid.,* p. 60.

20. Elaine Hedges and Ingrid Wendt, *In Her Own Image: Women Working in the Arts* (Old Westbury, NY: The Feminist Press, 1980), p. 289.

21. Eleanor Munro, *The Originals: American Women Artists* (New York: Simon and Schuster, 1979), p. 410.

22. Cindy Nemser, "Conversation with Audrey Flack," *ARTS Magazine* vol. 48 (February 1974), p. 34.

23. John Perrault, "A Painting That Is Difficult to Forget," *Art News* 77 (April 1978), pp. 150–51.

Annotated Bibliography

GENERAL WORKS ON THE HISTORY OF WOMEN ARTISTS

Recent widespread interest in women artists has stimulated the publication of a number of books in English about this topic. However, writings on the history of women artists date back to the nineteenth century, so three early treatments of the topic are included here. I strongly recommend all of the following for further reading:

BACHMANN, D., AND S. PILAND, EDS., *Women Artists: An Historical, Contemporary and Feminist Bibliography*. New Jersey and London: Scarecrow Press, 1978. A thorough listing of references on this subject.

BROUDE, NORMA, AND MARY D. GARRARD, EDS., *Feminism and Art History: Questioning the Litany*. New York: Harper and Row, 1982. A collection of scholarly articles that employs various methodological approaches, including analyses of works by women artists, to correct male-biased views of mainstream art history.

CLEMENT, CLARA ERSKINE, *Women in Fine Arts from the Seventh Century B.C. to the Twentieth Century*. Boston: Houghton Mifflin, 1904; reissued by Hacker Art Books, 1974. Provides interesting historical perspective.

ELLET, ELIZABETH FRIES LUMMIS, *Women Artists In All Ages and Countries*. New York: Harper and Co., 1859. An important early treatment of the subject.

FINE, ELSA HONIG, *Women and Art: A History of Women Painters and Sculptors from the Renaissance to the 20th Century*. Montclair, NJ: Abner Schram, 1978. Includes brief, interesting discussions of many artists. Each chapter is introduced with a concise, useful summary of women's social history. Useful bibliography.

GREER, GERMAINE, *The Obstacle Race: The Fortunes of Women Painters and Their Work*. New York: Farrar, Straus, Giroux, 1979. Contains useful information about a vast number of women artists. More important, Greer arranges the factors that prevented more women from achieving greater success in the visual arts into a series of obstacles and supports them with specific examples.

HARRIS, ANN SUTHERLAND, AND LINDA NOCHLIN, *Women Artists: 1550–1950*. New York: Alfred A. Knopf, 1976. A major source for the subject. Written as a catalogue for a traveling exhibition, the introductory essays provide informative overviews, and the catalogue entries contain pertinent data on individual creators. Useful bibliography.

LOEB, JUDY, ED., *Feminist Collage: Educating Women in the Visual Arts*. New York: Columbia University Press, 1982. Collection of essays on both specific women artists and broader feminist topics.

MUNSTERBERG, HUGO, *The History of Women Artists*. New York: Clarkson N. Potter, 1975. Includes discussions of women artists in prehistoric, antique, and primitive civilizations, as well as chapters on graphic artists and photographers.

NOCHLIN, LINDA., "Why Have There Been No Great Women Artists?" in *Art and Sexual Politics*, ed. Thomas B. Hess and Elizabeth C. Baker. New York: Collier, 1971. Pioneer essay analyzing the theoretical reasons for the smaller absolute number of women artists and the absence of recognition of their achievements in the mainstream of contemporary art history.

PARKER, ROZSIKA, AND GRISELDA POLLACK, *Old Mistresses: Women, Art and Ideology*. New York: Pantheon Books, 1981. A thorough discussion of the stereotyping of women's art, ideological preconceptions of the discipline of art history, and women's relation to artistic and social structures. Avoiding biographical discussions, these English feminists present the first serious analysis of the relationship between the historical evaluation of women's art and the underlying criteria of the academic discipline of art history.

PETERSEN, KAREN, AND J. J. WILSON, *Women Artists: Recognition and Reappraisal From the Early Middle Ages to the Twentieth Century*. New York: Harper Colophon Books, 1976. Contains a chapter on Chinese artists and many black and white reproductions. The text, however, tends to be superficial and is not consistently reliable. Useful bibliography.

RUBENSTEIN, CHARLOTTE STREIFFER, *American Women Artists: From Early Indian Times to the Present*. Boston: G.K. Hall, 1982. Employs an encyclopedic approach and contains brief discussions of hundreds of artists.

SPARROW, WALTER., *Women Painters of the World*. London: Hodder and Stoughton, 1905. Contemporary with Clement's volume, Sparrow's work is equally extensive.

TUFTS, ELEANOR., *Our Hidden Heritage: Five Centuries of Women Artists*. New York: Paddington Press, 1974. Lively biographical essays of twenty-two major women artists.

GENERAL WORKS ON WOMEN'S HISTORY

The following four collections of essays contain useful and reliable scholarship on women's history and span specific historical periods.

BRIDENTHAL, RENATE, AND CLAUDIA KOONZ, EDS., *Becoming Visible: Women in European History*. Boston: Houghton Mifflin, 1977.

CARROLL, BERENICE A., *Liberating Women's History*. Urbana: University of Illinois Press, 1976.

HARTMAN, MARY, AND LOUISE BANNER, EDS., *Clio's Consciousness Raised*. New York: Harper Colophon Books, 1974.

ROSALDO, MICHELLE ZIMBALIST, AND LOUISE LAMPHERE, EDS., *Woman, Culture and Society*. Stanford, CA: Stanford University Press, 1974.

CHAPTER 1

BOCCACCIO, GIOVANNI, *Concerning Famous Women*, trans. and ed. G. A. Guarino. New Brunswick, NJ: Rutgers University Press, 1963. Renaissance source for information contained in Pliny.

ELDERKIN, KATE McK., "The Contribution of Women to Ornament in Antiquity," in *Classical Studies Presented to Edward Capps*. Princeton, NJ: Princeton University Press, 1936. The only extant essay focusing exclusively on the role of women artists in antiquity.

JEX-BLACK, K., AND E. SELLERS, TRANS., *The Elder Pliny's Chapters on the History of Art*. Chicago: Argonaut, 1968; photocopy of the 1896 original. What we know of women artists in antiquity rests exclusively on the Roman historian Pliny's brief mention of a few individuals, reprinted in this text.

POMEROY, SARAH B., *Goddesses, Whores, Wives and Slaves: Women in Classical Antiquity*. New York: Schocken Books, 1975. The most reliable and readable source of information concerning women in ancient Greece and Rome.

REITER, RAYNA R., ED., *Toward an Anthropology of Women*. New York and London: Monthly Review Press, 1975. Collection of essays exploring the roles of women in prehistoric and primitive societies, pertinent to the issue of matriarchies.

SEIBERT, ILSE., *Women in the Ancient Near East,* trans. Marianne Herzfeld. New York: Abner Schram, 1974. Clear, concise analysis of the position of women in the ancient Near East.

ZINSERLING, VERENA, *Women in Greece and Rome,* trans. L. A. Jones. New York: Abner Schram, 1973. More concise than the Pomeroy book, this text deals with the same subject.

CHAPTER 2

CARR, ANNEMARIE WEYL, "Women Artists in the Middle Ages," *Feminist Art Journal* V, no. 1, 1976. Summary of available information on women artists of the Middle Ages.

CHRISTIE, A. G. I., *English Medieval Embroidery*. Oxford: Clarendon Press, 1938. Still the basic reference tool for *opus anglicanum*.

HARKSEN, SIBYLLE, *Women in the Middle Ages,* trans. Marianne Herzfeld. New York: Abner Schram, 1975. Reliable source addressing the role and position of women in medieval society.

MINER, DOROTHY, *Anastaise and Her Sisters*. Baltimore, MD: Walters Art Gallery, 1974. Brief but thoroughly documented source of information on women artists in the Middle Ages.

MOREWEDGE, ROSEMARIE THEE, ED., *The Role of Women in the Middle Ages*. Albany: The State University of New York Press, 1975. Collection of authoritative essays on the topic.

POWER, EILEEN, *Medieval Women,* ed. M. M. Postan. London: Cambridge University Press, 1975. Reliable source addressing the role and position of women in medieval society.

STENTON, F., ED., *The Bayeux Tapestry*. London: Phaidon Press, 1957. Standard source for the study of this art work.

STUARD, SUSAN MOSHER, ED., *Women in Medieval Society*. Philadelphia: The University of Pennsylvania Press, 1977. Collection of authoritative essays on the topic.

CHAPTER 3

KELSO, RUTH, *Doctrine for the Lady of the Renaissance*. Urbana: University of Illinois Press, 1956. The fundamental scholarly source for information regarding the position and socially approved roles of women during the Italian Renaissance.

SACHS, HANNELORE, *The Renaissance Woman,* trans. Marianne Herzfeld. New York: McGraw-Hill, 1971. A concise discussion of the position of women in northern Europe during this epoch.

CHAPTER 4

BISSELL, R. WARD, "Artemisia Gentileschi: A New Documented Chronology," *Art Bulletin* L, 1968, pp. 153–68. The first authoritative modern study. Contains valuable information and a number of black and white illustrations of less familiar paintings by the artist.

GARRARD, MARY, "Artemisia and Susanna," in *Feminism and Art History: Questioning the Litany,* ed. Norma Broude and Mary D. Garrard. New York: Harper and Row, Icon Editions, 1982. Scholarly article about Gentileschi's *Susanna and the Elders.*

GARRARD, MARY, "Artemisia Gentileschi's *Self-Portrait as the Allegory of Painting,*" *Art Bulletin,* March 1980. Scholarly article about a specific painting by Gentileschi.

MOIR, ALFRED, *The Italian Followers of Caravaggio.* Cambridge, MA: Harvard University Press, 1967. Sets the oeuvre of Artemisia Gentileschi into an historical context.

CHAPTER 5

GRANT, MAURICE H., *Rachel Ruysch: 1664–1750.* Leigh-on-Sea: F. Lewis, 1956. Short biographical essay with a substantial number of black and white illustrations.

GREINDL, E., *Les Peintres flamands de nature morte au XVII siecle.* Brussels: Elsevier, 1956. Study of Flemish still life and flower painting.

HOFRICHTER, FRIMA FOX, "Judith Leyster's *Proposition,*" *Feminist Art Journal,* 1975; reprinted in *Feminism and Art History,* ed. Broude and Garrard. Scholarly article about a specific painting by this artist, written by an author who has done extensive research on Leyster.

MITCHELL, PETER, *European Flower Painters.* London: Adam and Charles Black, 1973. Study of Flemish still life and flower painting.

RUCKER, ELIZABETH , *Maria Sibylla Merian: 1647–1717.* A catalogue for an exhibition at the Germanisches Nationalmuseum in Nuremburg in 1967, this is the most recent and authoritative study of Merian's works.

CHAPTER 6

BAILLIO, JOSEPH, "*Marie-Antoinette et ses enfants* par Mme. Vigée Le Brun," *L'Oeil,* March and May 1981. In addition to this scholarly article about a specific painting by the artist, Baillio is the author of the recent catalogue published concurrently with an important exhibition of Vigée-Lebrun's paintings, held at the Kimball Art Museum, Fort Worth, Texas, in 1982.

COLDING, TORBEN HOLCH, *Aspects of Miniature Painting: Its Origins and Development.* Copenhagen: Ejnar Munksgaard, 1953. Authoritative work that discusses Rosalba Carriera's contribution to the history of miniature painting.

GATTO, GABRIELLE, "Per la cronologia di Rosalba Carriera," *Arte veneta* XXV, 1971, pp. 182–93. Recent research on the dating of Carriera's works.

HELM, WILLIAM H., *Vigée-Lebrun: Her Life and Friendships.* London: Hutchinson and Co., 1916. Biographical monograph.

ROLAND-MICHEL, MARIANNE, *Anne Vallayer-Coster*. Paris, 1970. A thorough and reliable monograph about the artist containing valuable information not only on Vallayer-Coster, but also on her immediate artistic environment and her relationships with contemporary French still life painters.

CHAPTER 7

Angelika Kauffman und ihre Zeitgenossen. Bregenz: Vorarlberger Landesmuseum, 1968. Exhibition catalogue of her works in their historical context.

CARR, CORNELIA, ED., *Harriet Hosmer, Letters and Memories*. New York, 1912.

CIKOVSKY, NICOLAI, *The White Marmorean Flock: 19th Century American Women Neoclassical Sculptors*. Poughkeepsie, NY: Vassar College Art Gallery, 1972. An exhibition catalogue, this is the only published work focusing specifically on the women neoclassical sculptors of the nineteenth century. Introductory essay by William Gerdts.

GERDTS, WILLIAM H., *American Neoclassical Sculpture: The Marble Resurrection*. New York: Viking Press, 1973. Includes discussions about the White Marmorean Flock, but is an overall treatment of the movement rather than a specific discussion of these women.

LEACH, JOSEPH, "Harriet Hosmer: Feminist in Bronze and Marble," *Feminist Art Journal*, Summer 1976.

MANNERS, LADY VICTORIA AND G. C. WILLIAMSON, *Angelica Kauffman, R.A. Her Life and Works*. London: The Bodley Head, 1924. Best modern biography of the artist.

MAYER, DOROTHY MOULTON, *Angelica Kauffman, R.A. 1741–1807*. Gerrards Cross: Smythe, 1972. Overly romanticized, though more recently published, treatment of Kauffman's life.

CHAPTER 8

CARROLL, BERENICE A., ED., *Liberating Women's History*. Urbana: University of Illinois Press, 1976. Interesting essays focused on the social history of American women.

FLEXNER, ELEANOR, *Century of Struggle: The Women's Rights Movement in the United States*. New York: Atheneum, 1973. Standard and most readable history of the women's suffrage movement.

TILLY, LOUISE A., AND JOAN W. SCOTT, *Women, Work and Family*. New York: Holt, Rinehart, and Winston, 1978. The most complete analysis of the impact of industrialization on women's lives. Using data from France and England, this study pinpoints the economic and demographic factors that affected women's work and categorizes the types of work women performed between 1700 and 1950.

ZELDIN, THEODORE, *France: 1848–1945*. Oxford: Clarendon Press, 1973. For readers especially interested in the position of women in France during this period, volume I contains a concise overview of the political, economic, and cultural situations of French women during this epoch.

CHAPTER 9

ASHTON, DORE, AND DENISE BROWNE HARE, *Rosa Bonheur: A Life and Legend*. New York: Viking, 1981. A recently published biography, this work examines Bonheur's life not only for its artistic impact, but also within the context of the society in which she lived.

BATAILLE, M. L., AND G. WILDENSTEIN, *Berthe Morisot—Catalogue des peintures, pastels, et aquarelles*. Paris: Les Beaux Arts, 1961. A catalogue raisonné of Berthe Morisot's oeuvre. (French)

BREESKIN, ADYLYN, *The Graphic Work of Mary Cassatt*. New York: Bittner, 1948. Catalogue.

BREESKIN, ADYLYN, *Mary Cassatt: A Catalogue Raisonné of the Oils, Pastels, Watercolors and Drawings*. Washington, DC: Smithsonian Institution Press, 1970. Fundamental research tool for any student interested in the work of Mary Cassatt.

HALE, NANCY, *Mary Cassatt*. Garden City, NY: Doubleday, 1975. Biography.

Paula Modersohn-Becker: zum hundertsten Geburtsdag. Bremen Kunsthalle, 1976. Exhibition catalogue with valuable essays by Gunter Busch and others. (German)

PERRY, GILLIAN, *Paula Modersohn-Becker: Her Life and Work*. London: The Woman's Press, 1979. Informative and readable biography.

REY, JEAN-DOMINIQUE, *Berthe Morisot*, trans. Shirley Jennings. New York: Crown, 1982. Recent biography with a number of color reproductions of the artist's works.

ROUART, DENIS, ED., *The Correspondence of Berthe Morisot*. London: Lund Humphries, 1957.

STANTON, THEODORE, *Reminiscences of Rosa Bonheur*. London, 1910; reprinted by Hacker Art Books, 1976. The son of the great suffrage leader Elizabeth Cady Stanton is an interesting, sympathetic, contemporary biographer of the artist.

SWEET, FREDERICK A., *Miss Mary Cassatt: Impressionist from Pennsylvania*. Norman, OK: University of Oklahoma Press, 1966. Biography.

CHAPTER 10

BOSQUET, A., *La Peinture de Dorothea Tanning*. Paris: Jean-Jacques Pauvert, 1966. Monograph. (French)

BOURKE-WHITE, MARGARET, *Dear Fatherland, Rest Quietly*. New York: Simon and Schuster, 1946. Exciting eye-witness account of history in the making.

The Cameron Collection/Julia Margaret Cameron, introduction by Colin Ford. New York: Van Nostrand Reinhold, 1975. Focuses specifically on a major group of her photographs.

CHAMOT, M., *Goncharova*. Paris, 1972. Monograph. (French)

COHEN, ARTHUR A., *Sonia Delaunay*. New York: Abrams, 1975. Monograph containing information on the artist's life and art, as well as many color reproductions.

DAMASE, J., *Sonia Delaunay, Rhythms and Colors*. Greenwich, CT: New York Graphic Society, 1972. Another extensive monograph, with numerous color reproductions.

DATER, JUDY, *Imogen Cunningham: A Portrait*. Boston: New York Graphic Society, 1979. Contains many reproductions of Cunningham's photos and interviews with people who knew her well.

GERNSHEIM, HELMUT, *Julia Margaret Cameron: Her Life and Photographic Work*. Millerton, NY: Aperture, 1975. A detailed overview of this artist's career.

GOODRICH, LLOYD, AND DORIS BRY, *Georgia O'Keeffe*. New York: Whitney Museum of American Art, 1970. Catalogue; valuable reference source.

GRAY, CAMILLA, *The Russian Experiment in Art: 1863–1922*. New York: Abrams, 1972. Standard study of the Russian avant-garde.

HINZ, RENATE, ED., *Käthe Kollwitz, Graphics, Posters, Drawings*, trans. Rita and Robert Kimber. New York: Pantheon Books, 1981. Monograph in which a substantial number of the artist's works are reproduced.

HOLSTEIN, JONATHAN, *Abstract Design in American Quilts*. Published for an exhibition at the Whitney Museum of American Art, New York, 1971. Discusses the relationship between the aesthetics of the quilt and abstract art of the twentieth century.

HOLSTEIN, JONATHAN, *The Pieced Quilt: An American Design Tradition.* Greenwich, CT: New York Graphic Society, 1973. Focuses specifically on the art of quilt making—the techniques and the relationship to American folk arts.

HOMER, WILLIAM, I., *A Pictorial Heritage: The Photographs of Gertrude Käsebier.* Wilmington, DE: Delaware Art Museum, 1979. This exhibition catalogue is the only reliable study available on this photographer.

KAPLAN, JANET, *Remedios Varo.* Unpublished doctoral dissertation, Columbia University, 1982.

KAPLAN, JANET, "Remedios Varo: Voyages and Visions," *Woman's Art Journal* vol. 1, no. 2, Fall 1980/Winter 1981. Discusses the theme of the journey in Varo's art.

KEARNS, MARTHA, *Käthe Kollwitz: Woman and Artist.* Old Westbury, NY: Feminist Press, 1976. A sensitively written biography with a distinctly feminist viewpoint, Kearns quotes extensively from Kollwitz's letters and journal entries.

LISLE, LAURIE, *Portrait of an Artist: A Biography of Georgia O'Keeffe.* New York: Washington Square, 1980. An overdue biography based on the author's personal acquaintance with O'Keeffe.

MAINARDI, PATRICIA, "Quilts, The Great American Art," in *Feminism and Art History: Questioning the Litany,* ed. Norma Broude and Mary D. Garrard. New York: Harper and Row, Icon Editions, 1982. A discussion of the aesthetics of the quilt and the roles these works played in the lives of the women who made them.

MELTZER, MILTON, *Dorothea Lange: A Photographer's Life.* New York: Farrar, Straus and Giroux, 1978. Monograph documenting Lange's career.

NOCHLIN, LINDA, review of retrospective exhibition of Dorothea Tanning's work at the Centre National d'Art Contemporain, Paris. *Art in America* LXII, November/December 1974, p. 128.

OHRN, KARIN BECKER, *Dorothea Lange and the Documentary Tradition.* Baton Rouge: Louisiana State University Press, 1980. Monograph documenting Lange's career.

O'KEEFFE, GEORGIA, *Georgia O'Keeffe.* New York: Viking, 1976. Monograph containing many fine color reproductions of the artist's paintings, accompanied by texts written by the artist.

ORENSTEIN, GLORIA, F., "Art History and the Case for the Women of Surrealism," in *Feminist Collage,* ed. Judy Loeb. New York: Teacher's College Press, 1979. An introduction to the major women artists of the Surrealist movement.

The Photos of Margaret Bourke-White, ed. Sean Callahan. Greenwich, CT: New York Graphic Society, 1972. Extensive collection of photographs.

PLAZY, GILLES, *Dorothea Tanning.* Paris: E.P.I. Editions Filipacchi, 1976. Monograph. (French)

ROWELL, MARGIT, AND ANGELICA ZANDER RUDENSTEIN, *Art of the Avant-Garde in Russia: Selections from the George Costakis Collection.* New York: The Solomon R. Guggenheim Museum, 1981. Exhibition catalogue; contains useful information about Liubov Popova and other women active in this movement.

Russian Women Artists of the Avant Garde, 1910–1930. Cologne: Galerie Gmurzynska, 1979. Exhibition catalogue focusing specifically on the contribution of women to this movement.

Sonia Delaunay: A Retrospective. Catalogue for the recent traveling exhibition; a well-documented source for information about the artist. Contains essays by Sherry A. Buckberrough and others.

WITHERS, JOSEPHINE, "The Famous Fur-Lined Teacup and the Anonymous Meret Oppenheim," *ARTS Magazine* vol. 52, no. 3, November 1977. A useful essay on this artist.

ZIGROSSER, CARL, *Prints and Drawings of Käthe Kollwitz.* New York: Dover Press, 1951; rpt. 1969. Contains a substantial number of reproductions of Kollwitz's work.

CHAPTER 11

ALLOWAY, LAWRENCE, *Agnes Martin*, essay in exhibition catalogue for show held at the Institute of Contemporary Art, University of Pennsylvania, 1973. A detailed intellectual analysis of Agnes Martin's paintings.

BOWNESS, ALAN, ED., *The Complete Sculpture of Barbara Hepworth: 1960–69*. London: Lund Humphries, 1971. A complete catalogue raisonné of her oeuvre.

BRIDGET RILEY, *Paintings and Drawings, 1951–71*. Arts Council of Great Britain, 1971. Extensive documentation is included in this catalogue of a retrospective exhibition held at the Hayward Gallery in London.

DE SAUSMAREZ, MAURICE, *Bridget Riley*. Greenwich, CT: New York Graphic Society, 1970. A valuable reference for readers interested in Riley's career.

FLACK, AUDREY, *Audrey Flack*. New York: Abrams, 1981. Contains an essay written by the artist and reproductions of her works.

GLIMCHER, ARNOLD, *Louise Nevelson*. New York: Praeger, 1972. Documents the life and career of this artist.

GOOSEN, E. C., *Helen Frankenthaler*. New York: Praeger, 1969. Catalogue for the artist's major retrospective held at the Whitney Museum of American Art.

GUTH, PAUL, "Encounter with Germaine Richier," *Yale French Studies* vol. 19–20, Spring 1957/Winter 1958, pp. 78–85. Rare source in English based on an interview with the artist.

HAMMACHER, A. M., *The Sculpture of Barbara Hepworth*. New York: Abrams, 1968. Reliable monograph.

HEPWORTH, BARBARA, *A Pictorial Autobiography*. London: A. Zwemmer, 1959; New York: Praeger, 1970. A valuable source for understanding the artist.

HODIN, J. P., *Barbara Hepworth*. London: Lund Humphries, 1961. A complete catalogue raisonné of her oeuvre.

LIPPARD, LUCY, *Eva Hesse*. New York: New York University Press, 1976. An extremely thorough treatment of both the life and work of this artist, interwoven in a clever manner so neither psychology nor formalism dominates. Lippard was a personal friend of Hesse's; this book benefits from their intimacy.

LIPPARD, LUCY, *From the Center: Feminist Essays on Women's Art*. New York: E.P. Dutton, 1976. A collection of critical writings on contemporary American women's art.

MUNRO, ELEANOR, *Originals: American Women Artists*. New York: Simon and Schuster, 1979. Contains biographies of many important artists, based mainly on interviews conducted by the author.

NEMSER, CINDY, "An Interview with Eva Hesse," *Artforum*, May 1970. This article reveals much about Hesse's attitude toward her art shortly before her premature death.

NEMSER, CINDY, "Conversation with Audrey Flack," *ARTS Magazine* vol. 48, February 1974, pp. 34–37.

NEVELSON, LOUISE, *Atmospheres and Environments*. New York: Clarkson N. Potter in association with the Whitney Museum of American Art, 1980. Includes text by the artist and reproductions of many of her works.

READ, HERBERT, *Barbara Hepworth, Carvings and Drawings*. London: Lund Humphries, 1952. Insightful introductory essay and many reproductions of Hepworth's works.

ROSE, BARBARA, *Helen Frankenthaler*. New York: Abrams, 1971. The main source for information about this artist; includes lengthy text and many color and black and white reproductions.

SIEGLE, JEANNE, "Audrey Flack's Object," *ARTS Magazine* vol. 50, June 1976, pp. 103–5. Interesting essay about Flack's iconography.

SWENSON, LYNN F., AND SALLY SWENSON, *Lives and Work: Talks with Women Artists*. Metuchen, NJ: Scarecrow Press, 1981. A group of recorded conversations with living American artists.

WILSON, LAURIE,   "Bride of the Black Moon: An Iconographic Study of the Work of Louise Nevelson," *ARTS Magazine* 54, May 1980, pp. 140–48. Article containing valuable insights into the meaning of Nevelson's imagery and the development of her style from the point of view of her content.

WYE, DEBORAH,   *Louise Bourgeois*. New York: Museum of Modern Art, 1982. A catalogue for the recent retrospective exhibition, this valuable resource contains numerous reproductions, an introductory essay by William Rubin, and a complete bibliography for this artist.

Index